THE FAMILY GUIDE TO
PETS

Dr Chris Brown

MURDOCH BOOKS

THE FAMILY GUIDE TO
PETS

contents

about this book 6

pet ownership 8

1 short tails 12

2 best pet secrets 42

3 finding a suitable pet 110

4 the best beasts 142

index 226

ABOUT THIS BOOK

This was never going to be an average pet guide. A guide to pets should mirror the pets themselves — different, surprising, unpredictable and attention-grabbing. I don't want you to buy a pet and then forget about it, only revisiting it whenever it suits you. And it's the same with this book — get to know it, learn from it, and laugh at my animals and the effect they've had upon me. Along the way you might learn about what sort of pet you are suited to, what to look for in them, as well as some advanced warning on what they might be looking for in you. Importantly, though, it won't walk out on you just when you need it most. There are lots of tips on how best to care for that ball of fluff — some that might even save you from pulling your own hair out.

Everything in this book is real. Real stories, real situations and practical and realistic solutions. I won't be leading you on with flashing photos of salon-styled pooches with hair as high and as scary as the cost of owning them. And I certainly won't be setting you up to buy a seemingly cute and innocent little pet that quickly turns into 'Timmy the Terrible'. In fact, the real inspiration to write this book comes from just that situation. The families that didn't know any better; those people that despite all the best intentions, landed the pet with criminal intent. For those people that I see all too often in practice, it can represent a 10–15 year ordeal. Sentenced to a daily dose of barking, biting and bad behaviour. But it doesn't have to be that way. So take your time, be guided by my experiences and recommendations, as well as your lifestyle and life stage.

All the recommendations and tips in the book are genuine and tailored to you and those special people around you. After all, pets are not a backyard accessory — they are the backbone of the family. This book will show you how fascinating, diverse, intriguing and downright amusing the world of pets really is. I want you to experience it like I do on a daily basis. So no matter whether you know your pomeranians from your poodles, read on. As you will see from my experiences as a kid immersed in a suburban sea of pets, to a vet put in charge of their wellbeing, the one guarantee you do get from pets is that life is never dull. But, if you would kindly answer me one question — am I drawn to bizarre pets? Are they drawn to me? Or, as I fear, are their 'intricate' personalities allowed to flourish in my company?

Chris Brown

PET OWNERSHIP

Pets can be so many different things to so many different people. And they have to be. After all, their job description is extensive: best friend, fitness trainer, shopping companion, couch-warmer, food critic and tester, door bell, along with the constant expectation of being a source of amazement, amusement and frustration. But no matter what the role your pet plays in your life, you don't so much as own that little mate, as share your life with it. Sure, there is often an initial purchase, but over time, that little creature will make repayments in its own unique way — to the point where their personality and presence well and truly own you. The benefits of owning a pet aren't all for the animal. What they give back during their all-too-short lifespan far outweighs any cost or effort that we ever have to dish out. You can't help but be a more rounded and caring individual from owning a pet. Just think about it:

Pets make us healthy

From a simple pat right through to a run around the block, contact with animals can't help but drop the stress levels, increase fitness and result in a happier, healthier you. Their zest for life and almost unending energy supply will become something you can't help but take on board. You won't have time to ask the question 'where does he get the energy from?' in between the running, walking, swimming and playing that comes as part of the pet package. When you see just how much a pet can lick the stress and eat up the exercise, you'll see why they're the ultimate personal trainer.

Pets teach us about caring

Despite some amusing attempts to do so, most pets can't feed themselves or take their own medicine. They will rely on your caring hands to help keep them fit and healthy. Very quickly they will become a true and important member of the family. So in the same way as a child needs to be fed regularly, kept clean, have a tidy house to live in, learn what to do and what not to do around the house, as well as get taken to the doctor for regular check ups, so does your pet. And like a true parent, you'll begin to get a feeling for what they need and when they need it. The key to your pet living a long, healthy life really is as simple as caring for them.

Pets teach us about life

A pet's lifespan is always too short for our liking. In their handful of years, we see it all; their birth, growth, maturity and their decline and eventual passing. In the same way I did when I was a child, kids learn about life by watching their pets. Sure life can have its good times and its bad times but it's always precious as no matter whether you're a Sea Monkey or a serious human — life's always too short. So live it to the full. Handling the ups and downs of the human world is made so much easier when those tough lessons have already been played out before a child's eyes by Fido or Nemo.

Pets teach responsibility

I don't know about other kids but when I was young, the concept of responsibility through keeping my room tidy was lost on me. However, it was another type of dog's breakfast that really made the point. The importance of doing a job (like feeding and bathing my pet) on time, every time, never really dawned on me until it was my favourite little creature that relied on me to be there. Taking on the task of caring for a pet is a great way to instil confidence and independence in a young pup of the human kind.

Pets teach us how to interact with other animals

While talking to the animals is a talent reserved for the movies and for those in no hurry for an appropriate answer, communicating with your pets in other more subtle ways is a handy skill. Pets seem to have a unique ability to read our body language, mood and our tone of voice, so that how we act around them affects how they feel and act around us. So having any sort of little friend does teach us all to have a gentler side. Pets are often extremely vulnerable and fragile when we first get them. It's only through soft, caring hands that they develop into the creatures we love and that love us. Learning how to interact and be confident with animals is a skill that can't be taught — it's something that we develop given lots of practice. And it's just so important for later life. A certain comfort level around animals is critical. Kids need to know how to approach and

behave around animals. Not all of them are friendly like our pets. And it is that initial contact with an unknown animal that is so critically important. The ability to be confident, at ease, gentle and not provoke any aggression is crucial. Dog attacks are an awful occurrence; however, many may be avoided by children knowing how to react. The important thing to take on board is that having pets doesn't usually cause dog attacks; instead they help to prevent them.

Pets teach co-operation

Looking after a pet is a big job. And no matter how much you would like to be there for your little mate 24 hours a day, 7 days a week; it's just not possible. That's why the need to all work together is so important. Maybe you can feed your pet their breakfast and you can get mum or dad, or your brother or sister, to help out with dinner. Then there is bath time, brushing, walks and medicine to give. It's a great chance to share it all around so everyone can enjoy the fun. Just make

sure it's your brother or sister that gets sprayed with the bath water, cleans the litter trays and picks up the 'business' on the walk. The most important thing is that no matter where you are or what you are doing, your little mate gets looked after.

Pets are the ultimate companion

There is no friendship that is more dependable than that with a pet. Standing on guard, they keep a constant vigil; warding off boredom and loneliness should it dare enter your home. Fighting it off with a run, a walk, a swim, a play or simply just being there to listen. And unlike us, they are seemingly always in a good mood. I guess it's what comes from living in a world relatively free of stress and the burden of expectation. The bonus? Well, spending time with a pet shows us all a way to forget about issues and stresses and see what is important and fulfilling in life. They seem to have a unique ability to put the world into perspective.

1

short tails

One thing will soon start to become clear. Despite the very best of intentions it's probably better to accept that you're never truly in control of your pets — nor will you ever be able to truly control their effect upon you! After all, it's their personality that takes charge. So don't worry about any ups and downs you might have along the way — it's all part of the experience. I have a feeling that reading 'Short Tails' should take the pressure off straight away.

The great mistake

Whether a videotape exists of this moment or not, I can't be too sure. Whether my family will ever let me live down the incident is equally unclear. What was I thinking? Yet another unknown. What is clear, however, as clear as that crisp August morning back in 1982, is that an experienced host of a popular kids television show made a mistake. A mistake that many years from now she shall still talk of as being a dark and cloudy day in her usually stable, yet accomplished career. For it was on this day in a Newcastle TV station the likeable lady known only as Miss Kim — that provider of all knowledge to kindergarten children — made an elementary error.

For those of you that never had the pleasure (or indeed, the ordeal) of appearing on *Romper Room*, allow me to fill you in. In Australian culture, it marks a transition, the 'coming of age' of a child from a toddler to a kid. It is to children what the overly long speeches, spit roast and flat beer of a 21st birthday is to a young adult. For it is on *Romper Room* that the motherly Miss Kim invites bright faced children — eyes dazzled by the galaxy of suspended studio lights — to discuss life as they know it. 'Can anyone tell me what their favourite colour is?', 'who can ride a bike?' 'children ... do we all know how to cross the road?', she might ask. It was a formula without fear. Miss Kim would ask the questions while shy,

squeaky voices would respond in one word answers. The highlight of the show came at the end when all accomplished kids would wave goodbye to the lens on legs while Miss Kim would claim somewhat fraudulently that 'I can see Michael and Jane ... oh and Peter too ... and there is Ian and Michelle and hello Suzy, I can see you too!', while also looking down the lens. Smothering mothers would look on from the darkened back corners of Studio B making fidgeting hand gestures of encouragement while mouthing the most suitable answers as they saw them. All the while riding the roller coaster of anxiety and pride as so many had before them. Show after show, day after day, generation after generation, the formula just worked. Or so they thought.

It seemed like such a harmless deviation from the scripted direction of the show, 'does anyone have a pet?', enquired Miss Kim. She had merely tossed up a question, expecting a dear child like young Andrew with his brunette bowl haircut to tell the huddled group that he had a cat. Not much more than that; just that he had a cat. But no sooner had the last word left Miss Kim's lips than a skinny blond-haired kid looking sophisticated in his chocolate-brown overalls took interest. Such an interest in fact, that the previously reclusive boy sitting on the edge of the assembled group sent pigtails, coke-bottle glasses and fluorescent green elastic

Penny, a.k.a. Slobber Chops — the inspiration for the romp on 'Romper Room'.

hair-bands flying as he began his quest for his prize. Nothing short of Miss Kim's microphone would be acceptable. His movement was so swift (akin to pulling off an old band-aid) that no-one realised what had happened until it was too late. Because there, among a field of startled and windswept children and one teetering Miss Kim, he stood. Clasping the pink sparkling microphone, he looked deep into the glass eye of Camera 3 and announced to the world that 'I have a dog'.

Over the top of the muffled response of the deposed host the fill-in continued unfazed, 'her name is Slobber Chops'. This was not her name at all; it was in fact Penny. Slobber Chops was the name that Dad had christened her with in the previous week, when, due to a rather chronic and drastic drooling problem common to her breed,

Penny the boxer had left a trail of white, foamy saliva on the walls and floor. It was a scene that resembled the whipping of egg whites gone horribly wrong, but had obviously left a distinct impression on a young mind. It was not the only thing about the dog that left an impression as for the next 3 minutes and 24 seconds of airtime, a monologue on the dog's flatulence issues was performed. Complete with Dad's analysis of what really makes her 'rotten' and exactly why the car windows are always down when Chops is in the car. Producers, cameramen, mothers as well as children, and a redundant host stood by and watched. In fact, the scene was entirely still but for the chocolate-brown overalls gesticulating in front of Camera 3 and the blushing parent equally expressive with her palms cupping her shaking head behind the camera.

When the credits finally rolled, dazed and confused kids were collected from the set by bemused adults. With the lights now dimmed, the self-appointed host was just a kid again. Scooped off the set by his mother they made their way to the nearest exit. But there, blocking their retreat was the show's producer. Apologies looked like being in order. 'In 20 years, I have never seen that before', announced the producer. As Mrs Brown started to explain, she was quickly interrupted, 'could we use him for the next show?', asked the producer to the surprise of all. A stunned silence descended on NBN studios. Could this be a good idea? Mrs Brown pondered as she looked down at her son. Then, suddenly breaking through the quiet, came a piercing scream followed by a stream of tears. The toddler that had become a kid had become a toddler once more, and quickly ran to seek refuge in the calm of the nearby toilets. Following one of the biggest tantrums the television world has ever seen, little Chris Brown put an end to his stressful TV career at the age of four and a half by announcing, 'I just can't do another one ... not today', inbetween tired and uncontrollable sobs. I was finally coaxed out of the toilets and driven home with the promise of ice cream and a reunion with my old friend, Slobber Chops.

The extended family

In terms of first childhood memories, it's certainly unique. Most adults look back and remember that first horribly traumatic day at kindergarten, or the bike unveiled at the 5th birthday as being that which curls the sides of the mouth skywards. But no, mine had to be of a dog — one blessed with too much gas and saliva.

Slobber Chops, along with the rest of the Brown family, called Merewether home. It was a place that couldn't decide if it was a beachside community, or just the outer suburbs of Newcastle (north of Sydney). Neighbours of the Brown backyard will recall the local area as being more of a municipal zoo. For each morning they would wake up to the sounds of a rooster crowing followed by the nagging bleat of sheep, reaching a crescendo with the distorted bark of a boxer as she manipulated last night's bone around the jowls while making her feelings known. Every so often though, the city-bred locals would be confronted with a new morning sound to digest along with their burnt marmalade toast. The 'eeh-orhh' of a donkey or the shrieking of a parrot would often raise confusion and interest over the breakfast table. For my father was, and still is to this day, a vet. And anything, and I certainly mean anything, that required round-the-clock attention would find its way to Scenic Drive. Looking back, it was almost as though Dad was fearful that his three sons wouldn't be capable of making enough two-legged human friends. So as if to compensate, the four-legged and winged variety were accumulated.

At various stages 18 ducklings, three cats (Snoopy, Mittens and Mischief), four dogs (Penny, Claude, Rosie and Rusty), three koalas, one wallaby (Wally), six sheep (Honey, Bambi, Aries, Barry, Blackie and Monotone), eight finches, six chooks, one rooster, one donkey (Pablo), one cow (Merv), one horse (Patch), one pelican (Percy), and one penguin managed to live in relative harmony. Not in peace and quiet, but in harmony. Bearing in mind the number of playthings I had access to, it's no wonder that I now feel a certain sense of guilt-laden pity towards those poor classmates and teachers that would be put through the ordeal

17

of my 'show and tell' week after week. Like grandchildren have to sit through Pop's regular display of the 'vanishing thumb' hand trick; so too would the young pupils of Merewether Heights Primary School have to live through the latest twist in the melodrama that was the Browns' pets.

As a young kid, not even at my 10th birthday, I was still a long way from being a vet. Just how far I was from being a vet was highlighted one hot February afternoon. Mittens, our 5 year old black-and-white moggie, was a friendly little thing and as my older brother Matthew often proved, she was quite athletic. Like many cats, she had the ability to always land elegantly on four feet no matter how high Matthew gently tossed her. Half a metre (1½ ft); no problem. One metre (3 ft); no worries. Even one and a half metres (5 ft), which was a full five times her own height, was met with contempt as she seemed to almost glide to the ground. He used to call it the Mittens Circus, and always away from the eyes of Mum and Dad, his two younger brothers (myself included) used to marvel at the sight of it all. But then on that February afternoon, with my brothers down at the local corner store, the Mittens Circus had an unscheduled and unplanned performance, under the control of a new ringmaster; yours truly. The routine was initially a carbon copy of the normal group of tricks. Simple high tosses and elegant descents. But then, with there being seemingly nothing that this acrobat could not do, young Christopher threw in something that Mittens had not experienced before. It was the somersault. To her credit, she maintained her aerial form right until the end, before the carpeted floor seemed to arrive a little earlier than planned. With a definite thud, Mittens arrived back to earth. And with a definite limp she departed the scene. The Mittens Circus had certainly come to the end of its performance season. Dad, who arrived home later that night from a busy day in the clinic, cast his eyes over her. A broken tibia (just below the knee) was the diagnosis. Mittens wore a cast on the leg for the next 6 weeks, while I wore the look of guilt for the next 6 months. I had, however, learned an important lesson that your pets do (rightly or wrongly) instil a lot of trust in you as their only protector and provider.

Soon after the Mittens Circus debacle, Dad's veterinary expertise was called upon again; this time in tragic and heartbreaking circumstances. Penny, the animal that I grew up around and crawled alongside, was sick. She had started to lose weight and sleep a lot more. Worryingly, large lumps had appeared under her jaw. Dad took samples from her and announced the news one day after school: Slobber Chops had cancer. The whole family was devastated. I was shocked and confused. What did all this mean? It was apparently a nasty and aggressive type of lymphoma so we were all told to have our fun with her now because she might not be around for too long. She would come for walks and play with the tennis ball. During one of her quiet days, she even managed to take her first ever wicket in a game of backyard cricket, while sleeping in the sun just to the side of the makeshift pitch. Backyard cricket was a regular event and contested hotly between my brothers. During a rather spectacular innings I spooned a shot only to see it land right in the middle of her curled up body. I remember thinking it was one hell of a way to get out, but walked off the arena all the same. It was the last living memory of Penny that I have. The following week I remember quite clearly coming down to breakfast to see a grim group of faces barely touching their cereal. Penny had died in her sleep, and now lay there on her bed quite peacefully. It was the first time I had faced death. It was the time I saw first hand that nothing lives forever. Those slobber chops, always dripping with drool, were now dry.

As is often the case with pets, replacing them is impossible. You merely ease the loneliness by getting another one. No dog was ever going to replace Penny, but the house just seemed so quiet without a little mate. So, almost a year after Penny had passed away, Claude arrived on the scene. Now, I'm not one to be judgmental on a breed, but you might imagine that a group of young, growing boys living in the suburbs of a working class town might be a little sceptical when Mum and Dad announce that you are getting a standard poodle. Our fears were quickly put to rest though, when a feisty black dreadlock-on-legs appeared and quickly found ways to endear himself to us. His cheeky nature was only enhanced when from deep within that curly black coat would emerge the whitest smile you had ever seen. It always reminded me of the way West Indian cricketers would light up a day–night cricket match by flashing their pearly whites. He grew quickly and turned heads for a number of reasons. Firstly, the sight of a 30 kg (66 lb) black Afro running down the street was cause for some amusement. Secondly, and most interestingly, Claude had a habit of becoming attached to people (and animals for that matter) provided they looked in some way like he did. And by attached, I am talking about more than an emotional connection. My best friend's mother, who also sported black curly hair, became Claude's first obsession. She was heard one afternoon struggling to keep her footing as she

Claude interrupting his busy schedule to pose.

made the short, yet perilous, journey from the front gate to the front door of the house. The plumber, with a similar shade and curl to the locks, suffered a similar fate. So notorious did this stretch of contested pavement become, that those repeatedly offended would call out from the front gate for an escort inside. It was, however, Claude's obsession with Bambi, the black sheep, that caused the biggest stir in the rather conservative community in which we lived. For it was every morning, between the hours of 7.30 and 8.05 am, that the courtship ritual would reach full swing. Kids on their way to school would pause to observe as they strode down the back lane, neighbours would be caught peering over their fences and my mother would sit at breakfast, shaking her head as she announced 'it's on again'. Claude was certainly no Penny, but he was special and entertaining in his own unique ways. And to this day remains one of the most attentive, loving and loyal dogs that I have ever known.

Brown's cows

Whether it was the need to provide three young boys with more space to run amok, or whether it was driven by a desire to get out of the city, my parents decided on a partial move to a farm in the Hunter Valley when I was 11 years old. Aside from exposing me to the wonders of life without electricity and flushing toilets, it enabled the first serious contact with an animal that to this day still fascinates me — the cow. And it was quite an introduction. The property encompasses around 70 hectares (180 acres) of green river flats with a cool, rocky creek running through the middle. As part of the agreement to purchase the property, 40 cows were thrown in as a way of giving us a running start at managing a farm. We had been assured that they were all pregnant and due to 'pop' at any stage. As a way of checking how close they were to calving, they were all rounded up and manoeuvred into the cattle yards for an examination. However, something was not quite right. One of the old red-and-white Hereford cows, already straining under the weight of an enlarged belly, had fallen down. And despite much encouragement, she wasn't planning on moving anytime soon. After a good check-up involving all the boys twisting and turning her in all possible directions, a diagnosis was made. She was suffering calving paralysis. This often happens

when a calf, on its way to being born, presses on the nerves that control the back legs and paralyses them. Due to the cow's immense weight, they will never stand up unless the calf is born quickly and even then the stress of the whole procedure can be too much. With the old girl struggling, it was decided that an emergency caesarean had to be performed for either the cow or the calf inside her to have any chance. Dad started the surgery with me in the role of surgical assistant. In a matter of what seemed seconds, among a slippery tangle of membranes and mucous, a limp mass was shoved in my direction while Dad started to sew up the cow. The calf was out but it wasn't breathing. Under instruction, I scooped my fingers deep into its throat to remove any slime that might be stopping it from taking its first breath. But still no response. The next thing to do was to stick my fingers up its nostrils with the hope of annoying it so much that it had no choice but to gasp for air and spring to life. But nothing. In the meantime, the limp calf's mother hadn't been strong enough to handle the surgery and sadly she would never see her calf that she had carried inside her for the past nine months. The only possible joy lay in the calf surviving. But there was not much more that could be done. In a final desperate and disbelieving moment, Dad asked me to do something quite strange in the hope it might clear out the lungs and start the calf breathing. So, grabbing the sopping wet animal by its soft hooves on the back legs, I began to swing the ball of muscle around like a helicopter. Among a spray of mucous and saliva like a summer sprinkler, and flashes of a dizzy and outsized child, the unmistakable sound of a mooing calf was heard. With both my world (and I'm sure his as well) spinning uncontrollably, we both

Bridgette in absolute disbelief that I think the hat suits me.

collapsed in a heap. There in my lap sat a suddenly invigorated and energised lump of a bull calf; his thick red-and-white hair still slicked back by slime. He was well and truly alive. However, being orphaned he was never to know his mother and the warm, creamy milk she was to provide. Instead he had to be content with regular bottle feeds from the same people that brought him into the world. After an initial settling period at the farm, he was brought back to Newcastle with his adopted family so he could have regular feedings of warmed milk. He had a busy introduction to suburban living — meeting Claude, negotiating introverted sheep, cynical of his need for extra attention, and finally acquiring the name Merv. It

was a strange name for a young bull, but one that he really gave himself. After all, it was exactly the sound he made with such effort, tongue protruding, every morning when he was thirsty. It was also due to the thick creamy moustache that was flung across his face after each meal of milk that was identical in size and thickness to that on the face of the Australian fast-bowler of the time, Merv Hughes. In the next few months, lanky Merv transformed into a stocky young bull calf, with a thick neck and a habit of playfully bucking and kicking his hard hooves into the air at the sign of even the smallest excitement. He even provided the first and only taste of rodeo riding many city kids from my suburb will ever experience.

Winnie — the adopted child.

You would be right to think that by the age of 12 I had a bit of a confused identity. For a kid from the coast, I had become as comfortable with the concept of cattle breeding as I was with standing on a surfboard. Through numerous visits to sale yards and country shows, I had developed a particular interest in the Jersey breed. To an outsider, they are a rather bony, awkward-looking animal that struggle to support their massive bags of milk between their back legs. To those in the know, they are a gentle, caramel-coloured bovine that is famed for its thick, creamy milk, shiny black nose and long, dark eyelashes. Whether it was out of pity, or as a way to support the obvious enthusiasm, I was invited to help out at the NSW Jersey Cow Conference in Lismore. It was a week-long festival of the Jersey. Over the wet week, apart from negotiating acres of mud, I learned the finer points of the cow; the importance of a long, straight back, good udder placement and a wide mouth that could eat more quickly. Armed with

this knowledge, I instructed Mum and Dad that all Christmas and birthday presents would be put on hold so they might be substituted for my one wish — a Jersey house cow. Six months later, while at the Maitland Cattle sales looking for some more stocky Herefords to graze the river flats of Stroud, Dad stumbled across a strange sight indeed. For there, standing among wild, muscular beasts, was a fragile caramel-coloured cow, shielding her young brown calf from the unforgiving sounds of the saleyards. To highlight her temperament, and maybe to also divert attention away from her sagging back line and accumulating grey hairs, the auctioneer leapt into the pen and began milking her there and then. She didn't raise an eyelash, even if her calf did seem a little put out. A lone bid was placed and instead of the cattle truck delivering her to a waiting abattoir, she arrived at Stroud that afternoon. I named her Bridgette. Her calf was called Butch, as despite his tiny size, he seemed to have a certain pride in each step he took. The next morning, after much anticipation, Bridgette was milked and the first produce — a small streak of bright yellow butter — was on show. The bugs that had to be fished out of the milk and the hour of whisking that finally persuaded the cream to become butter were forgotten. What could not be ignored, however, was Bridgette's back. It was still noticeably struggling under the weight of a near full and ever expanding udder. The only option was to call in assistance. So, we drove 3 km (2 miles) up the dusty road to the local dairy where, with the assistance of dairy farmers Glen and Jude, a rusty-red toned heifer calf was chosen to be the saviour. Looking a little unsteady as she attempted to balance her petite frame in the back of our 4WD, she quickly proved herself to be of strong character. From the moment that she was introduced to Bridgette (her new mother), it was clear that Bridgette wasn't having one little bit of the impostor. But persist she did, and in between ducking and weaving from glares given to her by her adopted mum, Winnie, as she became known, soon learned that drinking at the same time and on the same side as Butch was the way around the issue. And so as Winnie and Butch grew, Bridgette's udder shrank along with her disagreements with Winnie.

Swapping the land for the sand

With the introduction to high school came a sudden new demand. The need to be seen as 'normal' and even cool. Quickly out of public view went the RM Williams riding boots and the stories of dairy cows, to be replaced by nylon board shorts and accounts of the morning's surf conditions. Bridgette, Butch and Winnie would all be visited regularly, however, the only 'jersey' regularly talked about was the collared variety sported for the local seaside rugby team, the Merewether–Carlton Greens. Now all sun bleached and surf-savvy, time rolled on. Claude was the undisputed king of the backyard and he wasn't shy in alerting the neighbours to it. His deep, resonant bark would echo back and forth across the tiled burgundy roofs of the suburb. Occasionally, there would be an interloper to contend with. Claude must have been baffled at times as to exactly where these creatures came from. Some sported feathers and wings, others long, coiled tails and short grey fur; fortunately though, none possessed tight, black curls. That would have made life a little awkward and interesting to say the least. It was the arrival of a

new animal one night that caused more confusion for Claude than any individual ever had before. What was this thing? It had a slick black coat that almost looked like a rubber wet suit. Short, bent arms that looked like wings but without the feathers. A beak like a pigeon. And two feet that didn't look like feet at all. They were flat and broad with more rubber-like skin stretched across them. If it was a bird then Claude was right to think our treatment of it was a little unfair. For this bird was being run under a warm stream of tap water and sponged with soapy suds in much the same way as he had been in the previous week after a romp in the mud. Indeed, this was no way to treat a bird. As next, through the gap between the glass laundry door and its frame, wafted the strong, smell of pilchards and other slimy fish. They reminded Claude of the smell the high tide mark had at the beach. It also triggered some distant memory of when he had thrown down the food that remained in the cats' bowl one hot February afternoon. It was mysteriously thrown up soon after with Claude always a little suspicious that the wily old cat Snoopy had been the instigator of the prank.

This object of confusion was in fact a fairy penguin that had been brought into Dad at work that night. Its short, waterproof feathers were gummed together with oil and only a bucket of detergent could remove the thick tar. The penguin would receive regular feeds of fish caught in the ocean close by in the hope that they would build his strength to the point where he might again dart through the swells. After three weeks of cold and greasy fish (and Claude feeling queasy at each feed), the penguin gave all the signs he was ready to go. His small beak would busily poke through his coat, preening his

A rare moment in control of the board.

feathers as though expecting them to be rushed over by water. But how do you tell if a penguin can still swim? Well, a quick dip in the saltwater swimming pool seemed like a good idea at the time. So with his small rubber paddles flapping as if propellers, he dived into the pool. The penguin disappeared from view in an instant. He was still in the pool, yet his movements (which had the same predictability as an untied and exhaling balloon) were so flashy and fast that an exact location was hard to grasp. So it was clear he could swim. What now became very unclear was how we were going to get him out so he could be

released. Being the youngest of three brothers, I was naturally the first sent in to retrieve him. However, trying to grab him with two hands was like trying to catch a wet, leather football with your eyes closed. With my increasing fatigue and headache from holding my breath without reward, all manner of pool equipment was thrown into the choppy waters in order to assist. After hours of failed attempts, a final combination of a pool-volleyball net and a leaf scoop was able to herd the darting penguin into a corner where he could be grasped. Wasting no time at all, he was driven to the nearest beach; the salt on the air causing an excited elevation in activity and the propellers to whirl once more. Finally the crisp saltwater enveloped him and, after rising for air, he dipped under the waves and was quickly away.

Losing the rhythm

With this same winter finally feeling as though it was coming to a close, the beach slowly became the scene of pursuits other than penguin-releasing. The football finals were only weeks away which meant the fitness program needed a boost. This usually meant a simple increase in intensity levels on the once a week jog down through the coastal reserve. The run was always made interesting by the sight of Claude, his dreadlocks flowing, streaking through the bush, usually in the desperate (and hopeless) pursuit of a rabbit that had teased him by flashing its white, fluffy tail. He was the self-appointed fitness coach — the pacemaker who set a cracking speed. Judging by the way he chased those rabbits, you would have assumed there was a greyhound lurking under that black coat. However, on this occasion, as the pace of the run picked up, there was no zip in his step. All of the thick, leathery pads of his feet were finding it hard to leave the sandy track. Rabbits went about their business a little jilted at the fact they were not worthy of Claude's attention. On returning home, Dad looked over him. He had already noticed a dry cough had been annoying Claude and now this sudden lack of energy had raised fears of something more serious than a slight tickle in the throat. The colour of his gums, normally a rich pink, were pale and cold. Dad invited me to listen to his chest through a stethoscope which dug deep into my ears. The sound coming from Claude's chest was something more akin to a rum-fuelled Jamaican let loose on a drum, rather than what I assumed to be a normal heartbeat. The sound was chaotic, rapid and harsh. An x-ray later that day confirmed what Dad had feared. Claude, my curly-haired companion, had a heart condition — a dilated cardiomyopathy. His heart was failing to keep up with what his body was asking it to do. The result was a shortness of breath and a lack of blood supply to his body, which caused pale gums, cold paws and constant tiredness. Suddenly, he was not patrolling the backyard. His bark did not travel across the neighbourhood at the mere mention of a visitor. And sadly, breakfast time was spent looking pitifully at him moping around the kitchen, rather than looking on in amusement at his 'extra-curricular activities' with the sheep. Dad tried a number of medications; some to decrease the extra fluid that was building up in his body, some to decrease his blood pressure, and some meant to give him extra energy. From the moment Dad returned home from work until the time he went to bed I would sit beside him quizzing him on what was going wrong with Claude and what the medications would do about it. I couldn't understand how this problem could have come on so soon and robbed Claude of all his spirit. But, no matter what we tried, he was slipping away. He would rarely move from the cane lounge that sat adjacent to the front door. Guests would be greeted by no more than a heavy lift of the head. It was just deflating to see and I wanted to be able to help. Eventually when it became too hard to even raise an eyebrow, or change his stare around the room, it was clear that the hardest decision of all had to be made. It was obvious that the only way to help was to end his suffering: we had to put him to sleep. So with all of the

I guess I should bear the blame for at least part of Claude's eccentric side.

family gathered around, we said farewell to those brown eyes and, just as I had been 10 years before, I was devastated. Shocked and distraught that in just three weeks, my little mate had faded away. It was so hard to deal with this time because of the fact I had known all parts of him, right from the very moment we took him home. However, Claude was never the sort of dog that hid his feelings or interests. A flash of that unmistakable smile and you could know for sure that he was enjoying life. A photograph taken a few days later shows the victorious Merewether–Carlton rugby team. Standing in the back row, I wear a green jersey with a strip of blue tape wrapped around the right arm. It was my silent tribute to a mate in a blue collar that had left me a few days earlier. To this day, I can say that it was the demise of Claude's energy and personality that sparked my interest in being a vet. So in some strange way, through wearing the title of veterinarian, I still carry that blue armband.

The Phantom Carers' Society

With the mark required to enter the Veterinary Science course higher than the mark for Medicine, many people often ask what the secret was to getting in. This usually distresses me greatly as I am concerned I may have been absent from school the day the secrets were handed out. The only key for me gaining access to the vet course was the combination of me never having the ability to play football for Australia and being too tall to fit into a fighter jet's cockpit. The thought of flying an F-18 at the speed of sound with an elbow or a stray foot hanging out the side window seemed a little too strange. The often

understated reason is that I do have a small liking for animals, and was prepared to work extremely hard to get the required mark to get in. Although there weren't many downsides to being at Sydney Uni, missing home was one of them. It was always difficult to explain to Mum that the main reason I came home every few weekends was actually to catch up with the pets, rather than to see her. But I always considered it something that was better off not said. It was almost a necessity to get home to the animals, as for the first three years of the vet degree, the closest we came to seeing a moving creature were the bones and preserved anatomy sections that were wheeled into the dissection lab. It was a strongly theoretical beginning to the course, which frustrated many people. While staying on-campus at St Andrews College, however, a compromise was found. For one night, while tucked up in bed early in preparation for the next morning's 5.30 am swimming training, there was a frantic knock on the door. Waking up the college rowers and swimmers was not something done lightly — with the effects of constant sleep deprivation it attracted threats of a serious nature. One such repeat offender knew of the potential dangers only too well. He was renowned for announcing his arrival home from the nearby Uni bar by unleashing his stereo system and voice upon the previously sleepy corridors. When this same guy decided to take a few days away from college to visit some friends in Melbourne (and made it public) he returned to find out exactly how much his late night vocal tones were disliked. It had been decided that every page from the entire collection of the college's Sydney White Pages and Yellow Pages would be individually torn, scrunched up and piled in his room. The scene was dramatic to

Don't throw sticks for him! Despite constant reminders to do so, Phantom found it difficult to give up his stick-chasing addiction cold-turkey.

say the least. It took a group of 30 guys, working on a shift rotation, 3 days and 80 phone books to create a sufficiently satisfying depth of 2 metres (6½ ft) throughout the room. The final result is as close to what I can imagine an avalanche of scrambled egg would do to an average room. Fluffy tufts of yellow and white were strewn through the room. Page upon page of the Jones, Chois, Smiths and even Browns swirled upon each other to deliver the result. To allow the crucial final touches, that would render all his furniture,

bed and dressing table invisible, the doors were locked and crumpled paper was tossed in via a window. Overshadowing the rumours that a small, brown-haired first year student was never seen again after clocking on for his shift, there was a clear message. And from that time on, no noise was heard after midnight when training was in full swing. Still it was with some startled surprise that I woke and stumbled, as though drunk, towards the door; tripping over my pre-placed swimming goggles and towel in the process. Even with my eyes almost entirely zipped closed to protect against the stinging brightness, there were two objects framed in a clear silhouette. My trusty mate Brad, a friend who although now living in the city never lost his country-born optimism and enthusiasm, stood alongside a small, muscular dog that, judging by the glint and focus in his eyes, and the partly digested tennis ball at his feet, shared an almost identical drive for action. Brad had found the dog (and decided on the name Phantom) entertaining onlookers outside a restaurant in a Sydney suburb. Phantom had been fetching items as widely varied as table napkins and chopsticks, at times darting back and forth across a busy road. Obviously without an owner and with little regard for the Corollas and Commodores that launched past him, Brad had decided that Phantom would be best served using St Andrews as a temporary safe-house until his past, and more importantly his future, could be determined. In the meantime, there was important work to be done. Almost immediately, the tired crimson carpeted hallway, eroded in places, became the stainless steel examination table. A stethoscope was thrust onto the dog's chest, joints were flexed, and even the wide jaws were prized apart. Everything, bar the thermometer reading, was scrutinised. Although appearing to be only around five years old, he was beset with problems more associated with dogs dusted with flecks of grey around the muzzle. Arthritis and worn teeth were easy to detect, even for a fourth year student. And with a quick look at Phantom's life interests and hobbies, it wasn't hard to see how these had arisen. Phantom was drawn to the thrill of chasing sticks and tennis balls in much the same way as a poker machine addict fronts up to their favourite machine, coins in perforated pockets. Phantom must have felt

that twinge in his hips, knees and elbow as he launched himself after that furry, yellow mucous-coated mass. However, the fear of another creature caressing it in their jaws overrode any pain. Having a dog in a university college held other advantages too. For the vet students, he was a living, breathing anatomical model that could be poked, prodded and studied. Around exam time, he was the most sought after object in the place. Indeed, only the local GP that freely dispensed exam-excusing medical certificates to the arts students rivalled his popularity. For the many sporting teams, he stood a constant vigil at early morning training sessions (there were usually balls involved; hence the enthusiasm) and provided reliable support at the inter-college rugby, soccer and cricket matches. Even the regular 5 o'clock touch football game became part of Phantom's ritual. Never wanting to be seen to be playing favourites, Phantom would swap between teams regularly, becoming a valuable defensive asset. In truth, as Phantom saw it, we were playing with his football so that anyone in possession of it was fair game to be run at, tongue extended, whether he ran from an onside position or not. As time moved on, it was clear that after much advertising, Phantom's misplaced owners were not to be found. Unperturbed, Phantom became a much respected and adored member of the college. A committee was formed to ensure his healthcare, welfare and happiness — The Phantom Carers' Society. As was the order of the executive powers of the student body, Phantom was appointed senior status. This allowed him free reign across the college with full privileges. I do remember some first year students being a little put out by the fact that a stray dog was seen in the eyes of the senior students as being more important than them. Furthermore, at a late night meeting, it was decided that if Phantom ever went missing again, then the designated Phantom carer of the time would be sent to find him and not allowed back within the walls of the college without the dog. The same meeting also produced the declaration that if the Phantom carer had not fulfilled all responsibilities by the time of the dog's castration in one month, then the same surgical procedure could be performed on him. This was the amusing, carefree and frivolous way the institution ran. I guess this was helped somewhat by the fact that Brad and I occupied the number one and number two positions in the college respectively. It was incredibly hard to leave the college at the completion of the year, and it was actually a major temptation to bring Phantom home with me. However, it was clear by November that he belonged to the college, as much as the college now belonged to him.

Delivering the goods

The final year of the Vet Science degree took the 60 surviving apprentice vets to the campus on the outskirts of the small rural town of Camden, south-west of Sydney. It was an almost entirely practical final year, where all the textbooks and models were magically brought to life — real, moving cattle, horses, dogs, cats, pigs, sheep and birds. Classes dealt with ways to diagnose sick pets, best medicines, surgical techniques and even how to deliver calves when their mums were unable to give birth to them without help. It was yet another occasion where my mixed-up rural and coastal upbringing was of assistance. Aspects of my dealing with the first few hours of Merv's life along with the adopted family that was

Bridgette, Winnie and Butch, had a habit of flashing back to me at the crucial moments and providing confidence that what I was doing was right. In some circumstances this was an ability not without its pitfalls. The 'calving simulator' was one such example. In an attempt to represent the almost daily occurrence and challenge of a cow in calving difficulty, a structure had been constructed that would test any aspiring cattle vet's skill, patience and dexterity. Although, sounding as if on par with the cutting edge, multimillion dollar technology seen in a Boeing 747 simulator, the calving simulator was, in truth, a slight disappointment. Instead of the rounded, thrashing rump of a pregnant cow, a fifth-year vet student was confronted with a flat, 1 metre (3 ft) square plywood board, adorned with a round hole lined with industrial black rubber to replicate the birth canal. Sitting in a contorted position just inside the rubber seal was a calf; usually a still-born from a nearby dairy. As if in a desperate attempt to add realism, the board had been painted with the black-and-white or brown-and-white patterns seen on real cows. It was the job of the aspiring Dr Brown on this day to 'birth' the calf. That is, to deliver it head first, despite it being folded up in a difficult way as many calves are in real life. After using my long arms to reposition the calf into a regular head first, front legs outstretched position (much to the satisfaction of the supervisor), I began pulling it forward, slowly persuading it into the outside (slightly more natural) world. However, judging by the size of the hooves, this calf was no petite Hereford. Still, I was confident I had seen it all before and was sure that it was nothing that 2 litres (70 fl oz) of gel (obstetrical lubricant) and a slight tug, using a specially designed calving

A proud graduate of the Calving simulator.

working on their own expert deliveries, stopped and watched as if anticipating a special moment in calving history. Strange sounds began emanating from the wooden board and from the junior vet, as the pulling and winching accelerated to new levels. The large bulge at the posterior of the calving simulator grew bigger, and despite there being about 20 mm (1 in) of pine between me and the calf, I was sure I could almost visualise the outline of its round nostrils and large brown eyes. I cannot tell you whether it was the 40 litres (1400 fl oz) of warm lubricating gel or the 60 kg (130 lb) Friesian calf that I saw first, but it was with a definite pop and a dull, resonating thud that the animal (in an outstretched superman position) and accompanying liquid, cannoned into my middle, and like a slingshot sent me backwards into the solid brick wall that had previously stood on the opposite side of the room. Strangely, I felt no pain and didn't even notice the bemused faces of my classmates. Lying there, panting, covered head-to-toe in the clear viscous lubricant, I was surprisingly content and had an overwhelming sense of accomplishment over achieving what had to be one of the roughest landings on the calving simulator. It was then that I came to the happy conclusion that the experience was about as close to the act of childbirth as I would ever come.

Concrete cowboy

The remainder of the year seemed to move all too quickly. After five full years of study and countless exams, I was poring over scrawled notes and heavy textbooks for the last time. The rather more daunting prospect, however, was the decision I would have to make over the coming weeks.

winch, wouldn't help. But still nothing. More clear gel was squirted from bottles (that looked scarily like those that dispensed tomato sauce onto my meat pie a week before), while more tension was supplied via the winch. Still no movement. Beads of sweat had begun to form on my tense brow, as both my arms and the winch applied more tension. The previously flat and unlifelike wooden board had taken on a very lifelike cow's rump curve, as it struggled with the opposing forces from outside and within the simulator. Still more pulling and winching. The remainder of the class, who had been busy

This decision involved where I would take up my first job after university. Moving to the country meant isolation, but with the upside of working with cows; something I have always loved. Working in Sydney meant the challenge of dogs, cats, birds and other small animals, as well as the bonus of a close surfing beach, proximity to the dogs at home, and my own cows at the farm. I tentatively accepted a position at Neutral Bay Vet Clinic; a small but busy practice just north of the Harbour Bridge in Sydney. A few things dawned on me quickly. I certainly missed the contact with my good friends from my vet year. I also quietly held a nagging hope that someone with a rather large backyard in the leafy and rather affluent northern suburbs of Sydney would deem it necessary to invest in a cow or two in order to keep their pristine kikuyu lawn in check. Sure, it would eat a little more than your average poodle or shih tzu, but what about the organic milk and cheese possibilities? Surely that would mean something to the people here? Whether it was out of sympathy, or as a way of reminding me of the life that I had put on hold, a few vet colleagues did try to find a way of bringing the country to the city. For on numerous occasions, as they were up early tending to sick cows and horses in the frosty country dawn, they would phone through a prank emergency call, requesting my assistance with a calving in Milsons Point. Even though dazed and disorientated by the unscheduled wake-up, I was fortunately able to ascertain that given the fact that a cow had not grazed the Sydney harbourside suburb for around 100 years, it was unlikely that Mrs Barnes was actually there at all, never mind getting nervous about her Jersey cow's pregnancy.

Take away

This unstoppable urge to bring a country flavour to the usually predictable inner city way of life reached a rather interesting climax in the week before Christmas of my first year at Neutral Bay. My mate Brad and I had been at a loose end. The whole pre-Christmas rush was simply not our scene; crowded and hostile car parks encircling gigantic shopping centres, overflowing with frantic people trying to control wayward shopping trolleys. We were looking for a slightly different Yuletide experience. When it was realised that neither of us were in the possession of anything close to a Christmas present for our brothers, it was decided that some action was required. And what better place to spend a blisteringly hot Saturday afternoon than at the Narellan Poultry Auctions. This auction house, in the semi-rural outer ring of Sydney, was a cluster of poorly-ventilated tin sheds that attracted a unique assortment of avian talent, as well as a diverse mix of talent of the human variety of animal. All sorts of budgies, ducks, geese, pigeons and poultry chirped and squawked their way into a chorus of disordered noise. Breaking only to dip their gaping beaks into tepid water dishes fashioned out of old fruit tins, before re-entering the vocal ensemble. Watching on, with eyes feeding on the sight of the birds, mouths open, clasping cold soft drink cans, stood an untrustworthy group bound only by their intentions. Restaurant owners and market gardeners balanced recipe ideas with the number of notes stuffed in their sweaty top pocket. And there, perched in the middle of it all, were the two that didn't fit in. For we had only noble intentions for our potential purchases. One laying hen would be met with great excitement by Brad's younger brother (a 12 year old chicken enthusiast) on the family farm in Tamworth in north western NSW. While from my point of view, a nice Rhode Island Red hen would bolster the egg-producing capabilities of the backyard chook pen. The bidding finally started and took off with great energy and enthusiasm. First to go were an anxious-looking pair of well-rounded scarlet chickens — sold to a poker faced man in a white polyester shirt sporting the words 'Golden Dragon Take Away' in large orange characters across his back. Next up, three week old ducklings attempted to mouth high pitched small talk to each other, only to have it quickly lost among the reverberating racket as the bidding on their heads began. Their soft, pale yellow feathers fluffed, and their eyes widened with fear as the contenders lurched forward, more closely inspecting their delicate legs supported only by bright orange webbed feet. Then as the auctioneer's hammer fell on their plight, an unspoken agreement was forged. The auctioneer pointed in our direction followed by disgruntled looks from other bidders — the ducklings were now ours. With sweat now pouring from the auctioneer's reddening face, bidding on the remaining pens became intense. The three recently purchased (and safe) ducks were soon joined by two roosters, three muscovy ducks and six mature hens. Geriatric being a more suitable term for the hens. What started as a simple planned purchase of a single chicken with laying potential, had resulted in the ownership of a mobile farmyard which clambered for the best view of a never before seen city on the drive back into Sydney. The cooling sea breeze was a welcome change for all and resulted in a much calmer collection of birds that alighted from my car back in Neutral Bay. A plan, whereby another mate who happened to be driving a truck north to the Hunter Valley and on to Tamworth, which would see the birds in their new homes by nightfall, seemed simple and workable enough. That was until a blown engine set a real cat among the pigeons — or the poultry, in this case. With the only option available being to set up camp in the garage where they now flapped their wings and chirped contentedly. From the kitchen came large plastic dishes of water, clumps of straw were scooped from the garden, and extra feed was arranged. By nightfall, all was well on Brown's farm. With my neighbours still none the wiser, ducklings splashed excitedly in the makeshift pond. Overly clucky and elderly hens (with overgrown nails and wrinkled faces) began to mother up to these totally unrelated and minute creatures — their clumps of yellow feathers now beading with small water droplets. I drifted off to sleep that night to the contented silence of 14 birds dozing beneath my bedroom. Dozing however, was not a word that described me and the entire suburb of Neutral Bay at 4 am the next morning. The two Rhode Island Red roosters, each adorned with long crowns of thick cherry suede, who until now had been reclusive and timid, had decided between themselves that being open and vocal about their thoughts and opinions was the best policy. Spending a night in an inner city, off street, one car garage must have sparked great debate. For much like a morning radio talkback program, the two sets of golden tonsils fed off each other's insights to the point where the tandem crowing only increased in frequency and volume over the remaining hours of pre-dawn darkness. Broadcasting out of their basement studio, the double act's rants and raves reverberated around the city, bouncing back and forth from skyscrapers and opera houses. One listener, presumably one of the wrinkly old hens, was so engrossed and involved in the discussion that she felt she had to comment ... and laid an egg in the process. Finally, when they had debated all of the morning's politics and scandals, the sound of more conventional urban activities made its way to my bruised eardrums negotiating two shielding pillows and a doona along the way. The morning light had emerged. Dry-eyed and slightly embarrassed by what some of the vocal elements of my mobile farmyard had achieved over the preceding hours, I dressed and ate breakfast in preparation for the day at the vet clinic. Some boiled eggs somehow seemed to make me feel a little better, both physically and emotionally. At the vet clinic, the appointments were mounting up. My first patient was a male labrador, Zac, who was a slightly round, sandy-coloured dog from the nearby suburb of Cammeray. His owner, Stuart, had brought him in because he seemed lethargic on his walk this morning. To add to the owner's concern, Zac had been up all night barking, which was very unlike him. Zac's dad Stuart looked concerned. Heavy eyelids seemed to be trying to compress his eyes to slits, causing stress lines across his forehead. As he explained all his dogs symptoms and behaviour, one thing became obvious. That look on his face was not a look of concern, rather the effects of a lack of sleep.

'Why would he be up all night barking, Doc?', he asked, 'he's usually out like a light ... all night'. He continued, but with some hesitation, 'The only thing I could think of was...', he stopped himself. 'No, it's too silly...', 'What is it?' I enquired, now with some hesitation myself. Despite fighting the

A good old chook — clucky and lucky.

urge to say it, he finally couldn't hold it in any longer, 'I know it sounds crazy — but I ... I thought I heard a rooster crowing. You must think I'm mad!'. 'No, of course not' I said in a reassuring tone, 'but I'm not too sure where you'd go to find a rooster round these parts!' I joked, but felt an awful pang of guilt inside. The Narellan Poultry Auctions would be a start I thought. I was pretty sure you'd find more than just a rooster there too. That afternoon, to the great relief of the entire northern half of Sydney, the mobile farmyard resumed its journey up to the rural regions of the Hunter Valley and Tamworth. And Stuart, the owner of Zac, had a long, hard look at himself.

33

A vet's pets: first Rosie...

People always seem fascinated by what animals a vet calls their own. I'm guessing it's for the same reason that whenever I lie rigidly in the dentist's chair, I can't help but study the dentists very own white pegs; peering deep into their crowns and crevices. And I'd be lying if I said I didn't find the flash of an amalgam filling, or the remnants of a root canal, slightly amusing. I'm assuming that it's because when we seek advice from a person, we like to know exactly how they do it themselves. And in the world of pets, the choice of companion often says a lot about the actual person. What can you deduce about me from my pets? Well, you be the judge — and be nice.

Rosie Brown is a dog that is as far removed from the world of polished pedigrees and renowned bloodlines as possible. She is, in fact, the result of an unplanned rural rendezvous in the back paddock of a cattle farm near Stroud in the Hunter Valley. Rosie never knew her father; however, most of the cows and horses were only too familiar with him. He was a cheeky male kelpie who possessed a dangerous but notable trademark that gave him his name of Nip. This dusty-red working dog would sneak up on unsuspecting bulls and horses and place a play-bite on their back hooves, and be rapidly in retreat before the large beast was even aware the daring act had been committed. The only fault with Nip's technique was remembering that if you nip enough hooves, pretty soon you will arrive back at an animal already wised-up to the act. The resulting pay back that occurred from time to time meant Nip now had real trouble remembering which hooves were spring-loaded and which were safe to lunge at. Watching over all

this activity from a neighbouring property was a gentle and timid female koolie (a type of Australian sheepdog). Although blessed with pale eyes like opals, and a coat spattered with blue, black and white colours, she never possessed a name. She would, however, provide valuable back up to the pack of working dogs that would regularly move herds of cows between paddocks.

Rosie certainly had a unique, and in parts dubious, mix of genes from which to take her pick. While many dog breeders claim to be able to trace out the many branches of a family tree right back to greater than great grandparents, Rosie's, to be truthful, more resembled a hollow log for simplicity. It was with some irony then that nine weeks after that unplanned meeting of Nip and the koolie, an assorted mix of six puppies first laid eyes on their multi-coloured mother and their new home — a cold, damp trunk of an ironbark tree. The heavy lump of wood was positioned close enough to the veranda so that a high-pitched squeak of a thirsty pup could occasionally be heard over the cricket broadcast on the radio.

As the pups grew on a creamy diet of mum's milk, word of the log-full of dogs travelled a few miles up the valley to where Nip's owner was doing some fencing work on our property. It had been over a year since Claude had passed away so suddenly. We had often talked as a family about getting another dog, however, there had never been full agreement on exactly what would be suitable. You see, finding a dog that was able to handle the confines and control of city life, while being of some use on the farm, was seen as near

'Where's the action?'. Rosie in one of her rare stationary moments at the farm.

impossible. There were no shortage of memories of Claude's failed, yet somehow amusing, attempts at being a farm dog, to add weight to the argument. His most notable being when he tried valiantly to befriend a humpy-backed Brahman bull, only to be charged at and end up swimming for his life when he retreated to the apparent safety of the dam. However, these pups, lying in wait down the river, seemed to spark some interest. They were billed as having excellent cattle-working potential while being home-minded enough to be a couch-loving pet as well. So the only thing to do was to pay a visit to the farm down the valley and look in on the pups down the log. Interestingly, as we approached, the koolie didn't perform the normal motherly act of growling and tucking her pups under her belly, out of reach of any potential threats. She merely lowered her head, flattened her ears and slinkily snuck her way out of the back end of the log, leaving a mass of brown, white, black and grey paws, tails and noses to squirm in discontent at the sudden loss of warmth. It was a strange reaction for a dog to leave her pups so exposed. However, with the pups lying there, it was a near impossible task to play favourites. Not only were they all striking in their own way, but no sooner had you put a preferred pup down than it was enveloped in a mass of round, well-fed bellies and slid right from view. One pup that did continually rise to the top of the swirling colour mix was a small female. She was wrapped in a rich tomato-red coloured coat and gazed with bright, golden eyes that hinted at her father's sense of daring and adventure. As well, a peculiar tuft of hair sprung from the centre of her forehead, as though it had been fixed there with hair gel. Before the inevitable emotional

attachment occurred, we placed her back in the log and returned home. From the home in Newcastle, it was decided. Collectively, the family agreed that this young pup would make a perfect and suitable addition to the family. The phone call was made. But one big question still remained unanswered. We had never discussed prices so the issue was broached. To our surprise, the answer was swift and strong, 'Nah ... no money mate. What I could do with though, is one of them big bags of dog food you see in the shops'.

Unlike many dogs that are purchased under sufferance from the breeder following exchanges of large amounts of money and a probing interview, Rosie Brown was acquired in exchange for 7 kg (15 lb) of dry dog biscuits. Hardly a glamorous start to life when you look at it that way. However, it may just have been the most important 7 kg of dog biscuits that Rosie ever knew. For the day after we collected our new dog, the koolie mother scurried away from her pups once more as she heard approaching footsteps. Just as she had done on each of our previous visits. Only this time, the visitors were not friendly. They were an ugly pack of bull terriers from a run-down farm on the road out of town. Hearing the disgruntled sounds coming from inside the log, the pack of dogs investigated and silenced the racket. Rosie was to be the only surviving pup from the litter of six.

Oblivious to her lucky escape, Rosie grew quickly, raised on a mixed diet of city and country living. Her size increased rapidly, as did her speed. Her desperate desire to race the car from the front gate to the hay shed certainly told us that. One thing that certainly never looked like leaving was that mohawk on top of her head. Impenetrable to hairbrushes, wind and water, it is still an immovable fixture. In fact, the addition of water only seems to add to the effect; rendering it in some ways similar to the pointy end of a sucked mango pip. Alongside the mohawk stands her pointed triangular ears, always quick to convey her fears, excitement and interest. Much like a yacht's spinnaker on a gusty day, they would be raised one second and then dropped the next, then raised again but swivelled this time in order to track the sound of a passing milk truck. Her coat is a deep red in most parts, broken only by sharp switches to white around her neck, shoulders, belly and feet. She almost looks to be dressed in a reddy-brown hairy tuxedo with a white collar and shirt showing from underneath, topped off with white loafers.

By one year of age, a distinct personality had emerged. She possessed all the drive, unstoppable energy and intuition expected of a kelpie. Being stationary is not a concept well understood by her. Amazingly, the horses and cattle have come to see another side also. One that seems a little reminiscent of a red kelpie she never knew. Yes, the back of our equine and bovine friends' heels have been known to wear a nip from time to time. The brightness in her eyes and the powerful, piercing pitch of her bark are gifts from her mother's side.

On the ball

An entirely unexpected side emerged one day, while playing one of the regular games of backyard cricket by the pool at home. Rosie had been content to observe the match from the sun-soaked raised garden bed that lay alongside the paved pitch. Any dull moments in the game would be measured by the way she quickly diverted her

attention back to the rapidly disintegrating tennis ball carcass that lay clutched between her front paws. She had gleefully pounced on this faded tennis ball after yesterday's hard fought match. Like most suburban home-made cricket contests, the rules of this game were unique and specifically tailored to the particular surroundings and potential dangers. For example, a good hit straight over the back fence earned an instant dismissal as well as a loud verbal scalding from the pensioner couple that lived there. They maintained that their prize-winning roses faced instant death if a soft, furry tennis ball so much as landed in the same flowerbed. The other rule of note involved the swimming pool. Three times in there and you were out. This was a commonsense law, as any shot played on the off-side of the pitch that landed in the pool took a great deal of time and effort to remove, thereby halting the game for a large period — much like a streaker that runs on late in an exciting one-day international match. This particular game moved to a thrilling conclusion — my brother chasing my respectable target of 38, was 31 not out. The loud slap of a tennis ball on the weather-beaten and rain-soaked 1984 model SS-TURBO cricket bat immediately drew the gaze of Rosie's dazzling yellow eyes. Along with her head, the ears were pitched high at the sound of the cricket shot. The ball was hit right at the swimming pool. It skimmed at first, as if fighting the pull of the salty water beneath. But then it collided with the sharp paved edge of the pool and collapsed into the water below with a resigned 'plop'. My brother, Tim, hadn't even had a chance to grunt his disapproval, when a shower of orange nasturtium petals and pieces of expectorated rubber ball signalled activity of the most excited kind. Rosie scampered quickly

across the pitch; her nails grinding on the hard paving bricks as she sought traction. Suddenly she left the ground and was horizontal, outstretched and over water. Among a shower of white water, and in one deliberate and definite movement, she landed, turned and returned to the shallow end of the pool, ball in mouth. Lemon-coloured fibres stuck between her teeth. For her first foray into water, it was an impressive one. From that moment on, be it a stiflingly hot summer day or a raw winter morning, she has rarely been dry. Most interesting is the non-discriminatory way she sees a potential bath. A heated swimming pool is approached with the same pleasure as a cold and murky eel-filled farm dam. As a matter of fact, the greatest delight seems to coincide with when she has been freshly washed in the days prior to a farm visit. Slipping undetected through a herd of hot and thirsty cows, she announces her arrival by launching her sparkling self into the bright green water of the trough that stagnates in the midday sun, thick with algae. Large, parched cows, their long tongues caged in their dry mouths, can only stand and wait as the dog splashes in the worryingly warm water; taking great pleasure in her craftiness and slimy green sheen. And the on-running battle for supremacy between cow and canine continues. It remains one of those amazing quirks of animal behaviour that a dog like Rosie can willingly send herself into an icy stream in the crispness of winter, but then flat out refuse a bath in the unbearable heat and humidity of late summer. That is until, dripping wet, she must stand there with ears and tail down in miserable sufferance.

Rusty — the country kid easily adapting to the good life on the coast.

Despite having parents that were both highly skilled in the art of working stock, this trait seemed to have unfortunately skipped Rosie's generation. She seemed to be all about noise production and provocation rather than actually moving the stock forward. One day, after repeatedly hearing the high-pitched bark, the thud of free running cattle hooves and Dad's frustrated curses that followed, the farm manager, who was fencing at the time, delighted in telling Dad about a dog of his own that was apparently even worse. It was his way of easing the tension that was written all across my Dad's face, with its accumulated sweat and dark shade of red.

Then Rusty: the other half

This dog had been a real battler since the start. Mick, the farm manager, had reluctantly acquired him as a pup when his mother had been hit by a cattle truck that was hurtling down the back road, late for the local cattle sale. Without his mother's milk he grew thin. His only option was to try and suck any sustenance he could from the discarded and dry lamb bones left over by the fierce and unforgiving working dogs. Despite despising the taste, it kept his own bones from showing through his harsh coat, and he persisted. The other dogs resented his very existence. He was seen as weak and incapable of fending for himself. Without his mother there to defend him, he would often retreat to the nearby clover paddock for safety. Safety here was unfortunately a false currency. While he was sleeping among the sweet smelling clover one afternoon, Mick had been doing some farm handiwork of his own; slashing the dead clover with a large tractor. The dog lay there dreaming of the day when he might just command the stock all by himself, with the other dogs looking on in admiration and awe at his control. But suddenly an awful machinery noise woke him. As he turned sharply, the front wheel of Mick's tractor ran right over the tip of his tail. Even Mick, with earmuffs and over the sound of his tractor, heard the shriek and howl as the young dog scurried away. Just in time to avoid the hungry blades that chopped the very grass that he had been lying in moments before. The dog bolted away, still howling uncontrollably. When he finally came to rest it was clear that the tip of his tail was broken and contorted in a bizarre direction. Mick finally gathered up the pup in his arms, cursing at the dog for its stupidity. He lay there shivering, his eyes wide with fear. Mick felt there was only one safe place for him. Even a young dog knew that there were two places working dogs feared. One was 'dead dog gully' — an eroded corner of the farm where working dogs that were no longer needed met their end by way of a rifle. The other was only slightly less feared than 'the gully' — it was 'the dog box'. A flimsy, rectangular plastic box with only a few holes that sat in a small gap behind the front wheels of a semi-trailer. It was a box that a dog could be transported in between farms and saleyards. It was also a place for untrustworthy working dogs that could be contained within it and forgotten. The pup would be placed in here while his tail healed and while he learned some commonsense. So during the cold, lonely nights, or en route to a far away cattle sale, he would cower in the box, choking on the dust that was chucked in his direction by the very wheels that took away his mother's life.

When he was finally released from the dog box, with tail healed but now stumpy and deformed, fitting in with the other working dogs seemed to be even more difficult. He had missed the smell of lush grass but also missed out on learning the finer points of cattle work from manoeuvring with the other working dogs. He would sprint willingly back and forth behind the vast herd of cows and their frisky calves, but failed in being able to read when they might make a run for it. This proved a major frustration to Mick, as it set back the day's work when other dogs would then have to go and round up the escapees.

He told my father this as they stood there in the paddock. He felt as though he had given the dog every chance, but through either bad breeding or just plain bad luck, he could see no other option for the now fully-grown kelpie, besides the dreaded 'dead dog gully'. Whether it was because he felt sorry for the dog, or whether he saw a challenge in the luckless animal, Dad would never say. There may even have been some truth in the thought process that said Rosie, who at times did behave like a petulant 'only child', would benefit from a mate to keep her in line. Possibly, there was even some logic in saying that by combining the efforts of two dogs that did a half-decent job at working cattle, we might just get a full-blown working dog out of this. All I know is that whatever the reason, I arrived home one night to find a quiet and timid male kelpie at the opposite end of the backyard to a surly and definitely unamused Rosie.

We named him Rusty after the immovable red dust that seemed to stick to his entire body, right down to the deformed tip of his shortened tail. He put on weight quickly once the stress of the old farmyard left his veins. One trait was harder to shake however. The combined effects of a hard master, the dog box and untold oppression meant that even the slightest movement in his direction would cause him to slink his way to the refuge of a dark corner. Once there, his head would hang low in resignation at the impending punishment. The saddest reaction though, was reserved for when an object like the garden hose was held innocently enough in your hands. Fearing a beating he would shake uncontrollably while his tail curled so far under his body that it would almost reach forward and cushion his shaking bottom lip.

Aside from the emotional scars, I have never seen a dog so readily adapt to a slower pace of living. They say that city-living turns a country kid soft. And Rusty is living proof of this. Rather than running a gruelling 20 km (12½ miles) a day across the paddocks and along gravel roads, Rusty attempts to perform what he sees as being the city equivalent. Trying to sleep 20 hours a day. These vast, draining siestas are broken only by Rusty's desire to take a few steps out of his warm hessian bed and stretch. And stretch to such an extent that you could be excused for thinking he is about to complete the Olympic decathlon in a single morning. First of all the 'fatigued' back muscles are extended as he reaches forward and groans contentedly as his warm belly kisses the soft grass. Next, each back leg is kicked out athletically before a roll onto his back for a quick sideways flick of his spine. Thoroughly tired once more, he retreats back to bed for the continuation of his day's work.

It's a life far removed from the noise and stress of the farm. Rusty's dreams occasionally stray back to the barking dogs, churning gravel and angry diesel engines. But, it is only the sound of a distant two-stroke lawnmower that he hears now, and squadrons of white seagulls dancing in the calm blue sky above. There is the odd return to the country — after all, he is the 'other half' of the Browns' working dog. But the animals are more forgiving there than at his old home. As if in a bid to conserve energy, these cows no longer aim to break from the herd and scurry for nuisance value. They merely plod peacefully up the cattle yards for their medicine. Rusty busying himself by running laps behind the stragglers, barking occasionally and looking intently interested. Thereby creating the false impression of a dog at work. He knows that by nightfall he will be back in the yard at home and closer to that warm, calm place — bed. Many city people retreat to hobby farms and rural retreats for a bit of rest and relaxation. Rusty has done the opposite and thinks this so-called 'high-stress' city life suits him just fine.

Your pet

As you have probably realised by now, owning a pet should take you on the fast-track to fun and mayhem. The trick is all in managing the chaos. Do this and it's good times ahead. You can see that for me, getting close to managing the mayhem has involved an interesting apprenticeship. But, fortunately for you, there is a less complicated way to do the hard yards. The Best Pet Secrets reveals all those little things you will need to know from day one, to ensure that both your pet and you live safely, comfortably and happily for many days to come.

41

2
best pet secrets

Knowing the tricks of the trade is always handy. In the world of pets though, it's going to save you time, money and even heartache. And if your pet is going to be an accepted and valued member of the family, then chances are that both you and your pet are going to have to shape-up and sharpen-up. Coming up are the secrets to your pet looking good, feeling great, living safely, eating healthily, behaving well, keeping clean, fitting in and, of course, staying out of trouble.

ESTABLISH THE RULES OF ENGAGEMENT

It's a simple enough rule — how you treat your pet decides how they treat you. But you might be surprised to know just how hard it can be to know right from wrong.

Rule #1 Treat him or her like a pet and not a human. It is great to see people showering their pets with love and affection. Every day in my vet practice, I see people doing and saying the most amazing things to their furry bundles of joy. In fact, I'm sure that most of the animals I look after probably eat better and have a wider selection of clothes than I do. The issue is when all this attention begins to send mixed messages to your pet as to who and what they really are. People should always remember that pets are highly intuitive and instinctive creatures. In the wild, the most dominant and superior animals eat first and are able to obtain whatever they want. So in the comfort of your home, when they are given the same privileges as yourself, they may just start to believe that they are much more human than

'Red Card!' — Rosie earning a stint in the sin bin. Taking a social dog like Rosie away from company is a strong punishment.

their size (and shape) suggests. The truth of the matter is that they are actually far more comfortable and relaxed knowing that they aren't 'top dog'. Being at the bottom of the superiority ladder (beneath all the non-furry people, including the ankle-biters) means they have no responsibility, no stress and no need to continually assert dominance — after all, they can't get any lower.

Rule #2 Play with them when you want to and not when they demand it. You should make your affection and time a valuable commodity that you don't just dish out whenever your pet wants it. This may sound a bit tough on the little guys, but if you give in to your pet when they whine, bark or jump up at you, then you will end up giving them the message that bad behaviour gets pats and rewards. Having a pet that expects constant attention becomes a real issue because this can often lead to barking, digging and other destructive behaviour as a way of dealing with their boredom. You wouldn't give a child a treat every time he asked for one, and it's pretty much the same theory for your pets. However, a well-behaved pet that sits quietly and plays when asked to, should be rewarded. It means that when it is playtime, your pet has all its energy reserved for a serious session — I just hope you're ready.

Rule #3 Know the right type of play. If you've ever watched young animals play together, you would know that it gets pretty rough and is not for the faint-hearted. I am always amazed that they never seem to hurt each other with all those teeth, legs, tails and ears flying around. When you do have play sessions, make them short and fun. Avoid games that encourage any sort of aggression as this makes it more likely to reappear in later life. Hide and seek and chasing games with balls (not small enough to choke on), and Frisbees are great, but try to avoid sports that result in contests between pet and owner, such as a tug-o-war. I'm not saying that you're in danger of losing, it's just that the tension and force involved often bubbles over and can make your pet wound-up, because to them it becomes a contest of dominance. Remember that you should remain in control of the game at all times and always win at the end of the day. This shows that you are in charge and the person to admire and respect — not just another young pup to roll around with.

TIP

A good place for a 'sin bin' is outside, in the laundry, or in a bathroom. Even a large box can do the job for a pup. Just make sure the sin bin isn't the same place as where they sleep.

Play between dogs can get rough, so ensure you stamp yourself as the one in charge.

If the play does get too boisterous, ensure you address the situation. As hard as it is to discipline something so small and loveable, your pet is going to need to know right from wrong. After all, they won't always be little angels and can all too easily find ways to be far from perfect. A good way to approach bad behaviour is to think of yourself as a football referee.

If your pet misbehaves, then quickly look into your pet's eyes and say 'no' in a firm voice. This must be within 5 seconds of the bad behaviour (biting, growling, humping legs, and so on) to have any effect. Remember that timing is everything. This symbolises a yellow card.

If your pet misbehaves again, it's time for stronger action. As quickly as possible say 'no', then pick your pet up and take him or her to the 'sin bin'. The sin bin is a quiet, isolated place where your pet is put when they have misbehaved. You have given your pet a red card. Being taken away from your company is a big punishment for a pet as they are social animals that like being around people. The sin bin allows them to think about their actions and know that what they did was wrong. It's important that you wait at least 10 minutes before allowing your pet back into the group; and only let them out when they're quiet.

KEEPING YOUR PET HEALTHY

Vaccinating

Today, we know almost as much about how to keep animals healthy as we do about keeping people out of sick beds. Your vet can now prevent many of the nasty diseases that can make our pets sick. So no matter what your little guy may be, ensure you do whatever you can to prevent sickness occurring. Vaccinations are extremely important to prevent, or at least lessen, the effects of some serious and life-threatening illnesses. When given by your vet they are also safe.

For dogs

Vaccinate at 6–8 weeks, 12 weeks, and 16 weeks if required. Boosters should be given annually. In Australia, this may protect against canine distemper, canine hepatitis, parvovirus, kennel cough and parainfluenza, as well as leptospirosis and coronavirus. Check with the local vet about what your pet requires in your area.

For cats

Vaccinate at 6–8 weeks, 12 weeks, and 16 weeks if required. Boosters should be given annually. In Australia, this may protect against cat flu (feline calicivirus and herpesvirus), feline enteritis, feline leukaemia, chlamydia and feline aids (FIV). Check with the local vet about what your pet requires in your area.

For rabbits and ferrets

Vaccinate at 8 weeks, 12 weeks, then once yearly. It's important to protect rabbits in Australia against rabbit calicivirus. For ferrets, use a C3 vaccination that protects against distemper virus. NB: ferrets and rabbits are illegal in some parts of Australia.

Worming

Young animals almost always carry worms (think of that next time you kiss your new best friend). When they're around their brothers and sisters, it's easy to pick up the eggs and become infected. For that reason, its important to worm your pet as soon as it comes home and then every 3 weeks until they are 6 months of age. From then on, a worm tablet every 3 months should keep the worms away. Your vet can show you the best way to do this. Remember, all pets get worms and they should be treated — unless your pets are actually worms.

Fleas, ticks and mites

Rather than using smelly baths or powders, removing fleas is now as simple as putting a drop of liquid on your pet's neck. These new types of drugs are quick and easy to use. But remember, you can't stop just because you've never seen fleas on your pet — fleas can be found everywhere, such as on your neighbours' pets or on stray animals, and the eggs can survive in carpets for months.

Dogs need to be protected from heartworm from 8 weeks. But it's easy to prevent. Your mate can have a tablet, a chew, a 'spot on' or an injection. The thing to remember is that it's much simpler to prevent heartworm, than risk the dangerous and difficult treatment for it once they have it.

Ticks are something that everyone freaks out about. And it's not just because they look disgusting. In danger areas, ticks can attach to your pet and cause paralysis after only 3–4 days. This can eventually kill them, so speak to your vet about what you can do to 'tick-off' ticks for good.

Ear and skin mites are relatively common. Quite often, you will see your pet scratching madly, or their ears and skin will look dirty and sore. Ear and skin mites are easy to treat, so speak to your vet about the best course of action.

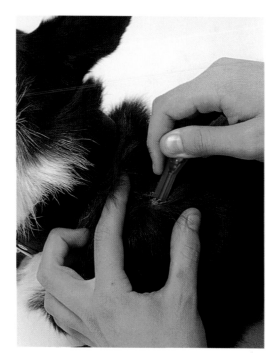

Modern treatments for fleas are easier to apply, and are a much more pleasant experience for your pet.

DID YOU KNOW?

Fleas are small and fast — making it near impossible to find them. If your pet is scratching excessively (and isn't on monthly flea control) then try this: wet a piece of white paper, hold it next to your dog's rump and briskly rub your fingers through the coat just above the tail. Hair and dead skin cells should fly up. After 20 seconds, move the paper away and examine it. If you see red–brown specks and streaks across the paper, then this is flea dirt — suggesting a flea infestation. You need to remove them using an effective flea preventative. Use a 'top-spot' (liquid on the back of the neck that disperses over the whole body) or an all-over spray that kills the fleas quickly.

DESEXING

Sure, just the thought of it makes most blokes cross their legs, but you shouldn't hesitate to have your pet castrated (if male) or spayed (if female). Obviously it prevents unwanted pregnancies, but it does far more than that. In fact, I reckon it's the single best thing that you can do for the health of your pet. Why? Just look at this:

- Desexed animals live longer, healthier lives.
- They have a decreased risk of cancer (such as breast cancer, ovarian cancer, testicular cancer).
- They are far less territorial and aggressive, making it unlikely that they will get into fights, be injured and pick up disease.
- They have a reduced urge to wander the neighbourhood. This decreases the risk of becoming a stray or, worse still, being hit by a car.

And don't worry, it won't change your pet's personality. All it does is reassign your pet's priorities a little. Before desexing: a loving and fighting machine. After desexing: a friendly, affectionate animal whose attention is solely on you. Desexed animals are generally calm and relaxed. Also, being more predictable and at peace with the world makes them great around kids.

I recommend that you have your pet desexed at around 6 months of age. By that time, they are mature enough to handle a day away from home but not old enough to have learned any bad habits. Desexing is important in dogs, cats and rabbits, and is crucial in ferrets. In fact, if a female ferret comes into season and isn't mated or desexed, it will die.

So, what's involved? Well, it's easier on both of you than you might think. It's as simple as a day in your local vet clinic. Your vet will give your pet a quick anaesthetic and perform the procedure. Soon after they wake up, they can go home. It's safe and quick, and with good pain relief, your pet will hardly feel a thing.

KNOW WHEN YOUR PET IS SICK

I bet you didn't know that your pet is actually an amazing actor? Like every animal, it instinctively hides any signs of sickness. This is because in the wild, sick animals attract predators as they make an easy target. So you need to know how to see through this performance so you can get them to the vet as soon as possible.

For dogs and cats

Be suspicious if your pet:

- is not eating
- is sleeping a lot
- has a lack of energy
- is sore to touch
- isn't grooming itself and has a dirty, dry looking coat
- feels hot
- constantly has its tail held low
- is unusually aggressive
- is limping
- has a strange-sounding bark or meow
- is coughing or sneezing
- is vomiting or has diarrhoea
- is having trouble breathing, or panting excessively
- has pale gums (they should be a bubblegum-pink colour)

QUICK LIP TRICK

If you want to see if your pet is dehydrated, try this.

For dogs: run your finger underneath their lips and around the gums. If it's wet and slimy, chances are it's okay. If it's dry and sticky like tacky paint, then your dog might be dehydrated.

For cats: pick up a fold of skin with your thumb and forefinger, and then let it go. If it doesn't immediately spring back, or just stays there, then your puss is parched.

Ever seen a dog or cat stick its fingers down its throat to make itself sick? No, me neither — I'm sure those nails and fur couldn't be pleasant. Instead, often the better solution is to eat grass. The taste, the feeling of it passing down the throat, and the effect on the stomach, all act together to deliver a slimy one-way express ticket to vomit-ville. If it happens often, and your pet is eating more grass than your average Jersey cow, then get it to the vet..

For birds

In the acting stakes, birds are even more crafty. They take acting to new levels. Look out for:

- a fluffed-up appearance
- not eating, or eating excessively
- watery or green droppings
- breathing with their mouth open
- not perching, just sitting on the floor of the cage
- an obvious keel bone (the ridge than runs down the centre of their chest, the sternum)

Remember that birds are small and fragile. You must keep them warm at all times and out of cold drafts. A hanging cage can be a cold and lonely place for a small bird that is used to nesting in a warm spot. If you have even the slightest concern that your bird is sick, then take it to your vet before it becomes more serious.

For fish

It can be extremely difficult to detect sickness in fish. It's mostly a matter of maintaining their tank well enough to prevent any disease occurring in the first place. However, there are a few telltale signs to look out for:

- floating too high or low in the water
- unable to swim horizontally
- white spots on their bodies
- fins that are damaged or torn
- any growths on the body
- rubbing their bodies on objects
- bulging eyes

When introducing new fish into a tank, ensure you check that they are free of disease first. Place them in a separate tank for a few weeks before they make it into their new home. This should allow you to detect any diseases present. In a similar way, any sick fish in the tank should be allowed to recuperate in a different tank — it might just stop the other fish also falling ill.

The most important thing to remember about caring for fish is that most diseases can be traced back to poor water quality. So keep a close eye on the temperature, pH, nitrite level and water specific gravity.

TIP

Watch the tip of your bird's tail. If it moves up and down, rather than staying still, then chances are your bird is sick. This is a really nifty way of telling if your bird is having any trouble breathing.

FENCING

It is your responsibility to keep your pet enclosed for their wellbeing, as well as the safety of neighbours. However, almost all animals are naturally inquisitive and like nothing more than to explore new areas. Bearing this in mind, a little bit of effort and planning will keep your pets where they should be. Aside from preventing your pets from wandering, you might just keep the suburbs' dogs and cats from using your yard as a holiday resort or even a toilet stop.

Microchipping

In addition to fencing, microchipping is a great idea to keep your pet in check. It's so simple and just involves having a little chip (the size of a grain of rice) inserted under the skin. If your pet is ever lost, then all the information about who they are, where they are from and who they belong to is contained on the tiny microchip. So basically, it means your treasured little mate carries their ID with them wherever they go. It's so important that it's quickly becoming compulsory in most areas.

TIP
Never tie your dog up near a fence. If a dog decides to take a leap over a fence while tethered, the result may be tragic.

Fencing for dogs

Sometimes you could be convinced that some dogs operate secret, after-dark careers as backyard excavation experts, contortionists and locksmiths. Such is the skill and stealth used to escape from a seemingly impenetrable yard. Bear in mind that there are four ways to escape from a yard: over a fence; under a fence; through a poorly designed fence; and out a gate.

You should consider that their athleticism is often underestimated — your outside fence will have to be higher than you might think if you intend to contain your dog to the yard. A standard perimeter fence is usually between 1.5–1.8 metres (5–6 ft) in height. Always insist on the upper limit if you have an active dog, such as a kelpie, cattle dog, weimeraner, dalmatian or border collie. But be aware that no fence may be able to contain a determined and agile dog. Self-closing gates are an absolute must and easier to install than you might think. Gate springs are available from hardware stores for a small price. It's such a simple way to prevent dogs from escaping (as well as keeping the kids in too).

Instead of a paling fence that has gaps in the wooden slats, consider a 'lap and cap' fence. These have overlapping fence palings. The 'peep show' that occurs between fence palings is often too much for a bored, inquisitive or anxious dog and may result in excessive barking and digging.

Anything positioned close to a fence will act as a launch pad. Seats, garden beds and even pot plants are as good as a ladder for a dog looking to explore the outside world, so ensure that you keep them away from the fence. If you're in any doubt, get on all fours and patrol the perimeter yourself. Have a look at what you would use if you were trying to get out. And why not do this in full view of your family and neighbours — won't that get them talking?

In areas of soft, sandy soils, it may be important to reinforce the area under your fence as well. Burying part of the fence may be handy to foil the attempts of any tunnel-based escape attempts. Sheets of galvanised iron are used in many regions for this purpose — they act as an anchor for the fence and as a way to stabilise the whole structure.

Always attach a 'Beware of the Dog' sign to your front gate — no matter how intimidating your canine may (or may not) be. It's important for a few reasons: it will be a courteous reminder to any guests (some of who may be scared of dogs); it encourages people to keep the gate closed; and will act as a deterrent for any would-be thieves.

DID YOU KNOW?

If there is a thunderstorm predicted, or a fireworks display in the area, your safest bet will be to keep your dog in the laundry. In cases of serious fear and stress, it's amazing what a dog is capable of doing. Most cases of lost dogs occur as a result of thunder and fireworks, as the anxiety invokes an incredibly strong 'flight' response. Turning on the radio will block out the majority of the noise. This is often not enough though, because dogs are extremely sensitive to vibrations. This is the time to load-up the washing machine with a basket of dirty socks and get it going. The vibrations and sounds of the washing machine will neutralise any fear-producing sounds coming from outside.

Fencing for cats

The ultimate escape artists, even Alcatraz couldn't keep a cat inside. In a cat's world, fences merely act as minor obstacles. The real importance of a fence lies in trying to keep neighbouring animals *out* of the yard. Remember that:

- Cats are extremely territorial and any challenge to your cat's territory should be avoided. Cat fight wounds (especially abscesses), and the spread of disease, are unfortunate by-products of fights over territory.

- Cats will mark any new territory they encounter. So if you're not careful, this can turn your garden into a communal toilet.

- Anxiety in cats is often an understated issue in our felines. The signs are typically urine spraying, marking, excess vocalisation, excess meowing, and stereotypic disorders such as overgrooming. A feeling of insecurity in their surroundings is a common cause of this behavioural problem — a situation not helped by repetitive visits from neighbourhood cats.

So, either keep your cats inside all day (or night-time at least) or restrict your cat to a well-contained courtyard. And:

- Supervise any outside excursions.
- Have a water-spray bottle on hand to spray any trespassing cats.
- Try mothballs around the perimeter of the yard to provide a strong-smelling deterrent.
- Try using one of the commercially-available deterrent sprays.

A cat enclosure like this is a great idea. It ensures your cats are safe and relaxed, as well as keeping other cats on the outer.

Why climb over, when you can dig under?

You are often better off just assuming that a cat will jump any barricade you install. Importantly, however, ensure that there are no sharp points, hooks or nails on fences. Serious injuries to the body can result from unexpected encounters.

For other pets

Consider that many small animals are excellent diggers. And apart from easily digging their way out of a yard, a pet like a rabbit will leave your yard looking more like the moon's surface than the lovely sculptured grassed area it once was.

Being small and vulnerable, many small pets (rabbits, birds, guinea pigs, and so on) know that being exposed is dangerous to their existence. They may actually be more relaxed when provided with shelter and smaller play areas. It may sound straightforward, but small pets can fit into small spaces. Don't leave anything to chance when it comes to containing small pets.

EXERCISE AND SOCIALISATION

After the question 'Do you think my pet is fat?', the most commonly asked question I hear is 'When can we take our puppy/kitten outside?'.

So when is it safe to walk, play and socialise your animal, without putting it at serious risk of disease? There are lots of theories regarding when it is safe. However, it really represents a balancing act between the potential benefits and dangers.

Socialisation

Socialisation involves making your pet more comfortable and predictable in their surroundings, which can only make them (and you) more happy in the long run. It's all about getting them out there and letting them meet and greet as many different animals and people of all ages, shapes and sizes. Socialisation assists in breaking down any fears, meaning pets are more predictable in unplanned situations. This comes in handy if your dog is confronted by a large dog in the park or when they are patted by unfamiliar people. It also makes your pet less defensive of their own space. It's important to realise that you only get one go at making your pet more social. You must socialise them between 8-16 weeks as this seems to be the time that they make up their mind on the world around them.

Exercise

Exercise is seen by many new pet owners as an important part of a puppy's first few weeks. However, we often overestimate just how much they really need it. The benefit lies more in the pets and people they encounter, than in the exercise itself. Even a quick glance at a puppy's average day shows that they exert a huge amount of energy in an average play session, and between these times are usually found sleeping. It must be remembered that young dogs (and cats) are growing rapidly at this age, so their bodies must be treated with care. Excessive and strenuous exercise can damage immature joints and increase their risk of hip dysplasia and arthritis in later life. Long runs and extended periods of chasing balls or Frisbees should be avoided.

Risk of disease

A young animal, only recently weaned from its mother, has limited protection from bacterial diseases and viruses. Their immune system is immature, which is why vets insist upon vaccinations as a way of providing a suitable level of protection. The main concerns for dogs are parvovirus, canine distemper virus and kennel cough. Parvovirus is a significant danger in parts of Australia where vaccinations aren't routinely performed. Not only is it potentially fatal, but the virus may survive for long periods before infecting other animals. Kennel cough is the most common, though least severe, disease to vaccinate against. This infection of the trachea causes a chronic, dry cough that may last for weeks or months, and is easily transferred by dogs in close contact.

The whole 'when to walk' debate comes down to an educated judgement. If you're in an area of low vaccination compliance, wait until the full course of shots (at 16 weeks) has taken effect. In most areas, however, you could wait until one week after the second (12 week) injection. My feeling has always been that with two vaccinations in their system (and the significant level of protection they provide), the benefits of socialisation outweigh the small risk of picking up a virus.

Puppy's first walk. Socialise your pets early for the best results in later life.

Exercising

Get your new pup used to a leash. Walks on a leash have the dual benefit of minimising damage to the joints (as dogs tend to walk at a gentle, controlled pace) but also allow a young dog to get used to, and be comfortable with, being led on a leash. Pretty soon it will be the dog that is leading you on the walks, so enjoy it while it lasts.

Make the walks short, as pups have a limited energy level and concentration span. Keeping walks to around 15–30 minutes will gently build up fitness while not damaging those developing knees, hips and elbows. Continue this until 12 months of age. Their body will have reached close to full maturity by 12–14 months, making more strenuous exercise a possibility at this age.

But remember that no matter how much your dog loves chasing balls and Frisbees, keep this to a minimum. The twisting and turning, and stopping and starting movements will put enormous strain on your dog's body, especially in the hips, knees and elbows. Early onset of arthritis (at around 5 years of age) is an all too common result of a ball-chasing addiction.

You should never throw sticks for your dog to chase. Even though most people do it, the risk of the stick splintering and causing damage to your dog's neck, mouth or stomach is an ever-present danger. Hard-wearing rubber balls (large enough so they cannot be swallowed) are a much safer alternative for your dog.

Any limping should be regarded as serious. Injuries to bones, muscles, ligaments, joints and, most importantly, growth plates, can hinder a young dog's normal growth pattern, so get it checked out as soon as you can and rest them until a specific cause is identified.

Cuts and abrasions to the pads and webbing of the feet are common and may require bandaging and medication. It will take many months for toe pads to 'roughen-up' to the point that they are ready to be run on concrete and tar surfaces, so take it easy for starters.

If your pup insists on stopping during a walk or a run, there is probably a reason for it so you should allow them to rest. It may be that they don't yet possess the necessary fitness for the exercise, they are too hot to continue, or they may be sore.

Dogs don't sweat — they lose most of their body heat by panting. To allow them to keep cool, be sure to provide some cool water during and especially after exercise. Shade and a cool spot to rest will be necessary in warm conditions.

Pulling too hard on the lead is often seen with energetic and enthusiastic breeds. Rather than pointing to a family tree full of sled-pulling huskies, it's usually a trademark of an over-exuberant dog keen to get moving and pick up the pace. If this is a common occurrence in your dog, it's important to minimise the behaviour. Try a harness that allows the tension of the lead to pass through the shoulders and/or the head, rather than the neck. Use of choker chains in this situation is extremely dangerous, as it may cause a flattening of the windpipe when the chain continually pulls over this area. It may also be worth encouraging the dog to walk alongside rather than pulling in front.

When you are walking your best mate, it's important to think about keeping mates with all the other people that use the same park, beach or track. Remember to always carry some small plastic bags for collecting 'the business'. Any old bag is fine provided it meets all the critical criteria: there are no holes in it; and it isn't easily confused with your lunch bag. Sounds simple, but it's a mistake you'll only make once.

Safety tips

When exercising, take special care with:

Heat stroke

This is where your pet begins to overheat and no matter how much they pant, they can't cool down. It can be extremely serious and even fatal. The early warning signs are excessive panting, drooling and shortness of breath. Your pet will feel hot to touch and look distressed. Heat stroke will affect any pet if the conditions are severe enough. Be extra careful on hot and humid days, and especially with dark coloured pets. Rather than reflecting the sun's rays, dark coats absorb it. Like a sponge they suck up all the heat around them. In warm weather, only exercise them in the cool of the morning or late afternoon. Shade around the house is also a necessity, as an animal can develop heat stroke just by being left alone in the yard if there is no choice but to lie in the sun.

Apart from exercising, be careful of heat stroke when taking your pet on car trips. No matter how much of a fraction of time it may be, never leave your pet alone in a parked car. The temperature inside a parked car can rapidly climb above 50°C (120°F). With no ability to sweat and no fresh air to breathe, the situation will turn into tragedy within minutes.

Flat-nosed breeds

The shape of their face, as well as the structure of their throat, means you must be extra careful with flat-nosed breeds (such as boxers, bulldogs and staffies). Their flat face means that the nostrils are squashed-up and their throat isn't wide enough to allow them to breathe freely, even on cool days. When it's hot, they really struggle to pant well enough to keep cool. So, try avoiding the heat of the day and ensure there are plenty of shady rest

Go easy on the exercise with flat-nosed dog breeds, such as staffies.

Be extra careful with large dog breeds that eat then exercise soon after.

spots along the way. With the strings of drool that fly from their face like untied shoelaces, it's easy to see why these breeds are prone to dehydration. After all, that saliva takes some work to produce. Never forget to keep up the supply of water.

Large dogs

If you're like me, then I'm sure you remember being told over and over again not to swim or run around after meals. And when you did, nothing ever happened did it? Well, now it's your turn to return the favour. Only in this case it is serious. You must always be careful not to give your pet a large meal or drink of water before exercise.

Dogs, especially large breeds of dogs such as labradors, golden retrievers, boxers, standard poodles, great danes, saint bernards, german shepherds and rottweilers are prone to developing

a severe form of bloat which can be fatal. The biggest risk factor involved is eating a large meal or having a large drink of water before exercise. During a run, the swollen stomach can twist on itself and block off any way in or out for all that fluid. The stomach then becomes an expanding balloon that makes the dog extremely sick.

If you see your dog with a bloated gut, trying to vomit, drooling excessively and seeming in pain, then take him or her to the vet as quick as you can. A few minutes can make the difference between life and death in a situation like this. These dogs are naturally playful breeds, so this condition may occur at almost any time. So be on the lookout for any worrying signs.

BATHING

I reckon we as pet owners are a lot like kids when it comes to bath time. We know its got to happen at some stage, but it's a bit of a hassle, and you'd rather it didn't have to be done at all. Besides, half the time I've given a dog a bath, I've actually ended up wetter than the dog itself. And as important as a shiny, flea-free coat is, I just don't really think it's the look *I'm* after.

Bath time can hold a lot of fears for the pet (and sometimes even the owner). But it shouldn't be something to worry about. If you can bathe yourself, then you can bathe your pet — it's that simple. To save you making an appointment at the vet surgery, why don't I answer the important questions for you.

Why bathe our pets?

We bathe our pets in order to dislodge dirt, bacteria and excess skin oils and odour from their coat. If your pet spends any time inside, then you will understand why bad body odour is the main reason people will seek to bathe their little mates. It's amazing how a clean, fresh-smelling little creature metamorphoses into a walking garbage bag within hours. It's a fact that many dogs instinctively try to make themselves dirty straight after a bath. That's because in the wild, smelling

FUN FOR BIRDS

Life in a cage can get a little boring for a bird. So why not bring the outside world to it. Using a very fine spray (from a water atomiser), give your birds a quick misting. This will keep them entertained for hours as they preen all the water droplets from their feathers. Be sure not to wet them or their cage excessively, as this may make them cold. Just a few sprays will do the trick.

like something other than the dirt around you is a big disadvantage for hunting. Trust me, I should know — Rosie will go and roll herself in horse manure the day after a bath and end up smelling far worse than she did before her wash. Sadly, I reckon she thinks she smells great.

How often?

Cats rarely need a bath (once every few months is plenty) as they are meticulous at keeping themselves clean through grooming (unlike Rosie). A good brush is important though. Birds are also very good at self-cleaning (called 'preening') and won't require a bath.

Almost all other pets rarely need bathing, except when there is a medical problem. Guinea pigs and rabbits should only be bathed on the recommendation of your vet. Often a simple wipe-down with a damp cloth is sufficient. For small, fragile creatures (such as mice) I would not recommend bathing them at all. Remember that your pet is most likely scared of water and may panic if put near, or in, it. Stress is a big problem for these little guys and can kill them. So basically don't freak them out if you don't have to. If bathing is really a worrying issue, then why not get a pet trained to bathe itself ... like a fish.

Dogs are certainly the animal most often in need of a good scrub. If your dogs are anything like mine, then they usually can't keep themselves out of trouble. Dogs should be bathed no more than once a week and on average once a month is about right. Their breed, the climate and the conditions you keep your dog in, are big factors to decide how often to bathe. Dogs that spend most of their time inside will stay cleaner, but owners in this situation are more likely to notice even the slightest smell and insist upon a bath.

Important oils

There are significant differences between dog skin and human skin that mean it's dangerous to bathe a dog too often. Their outer skin layer (epidermis) is significantly thinner than ours, meaning it's more easily damaged.

They require a certain level of skin oils to keep their skin healthy and to prevent it from drying out. Without these oils, the skin can become flaky and is more susceptible to infection as the bacteria can get under the fragile skin. The coat also requires oils to act as conditioners (just like you use) to the hair. Oil free hair will stand up and be 'frizzy' due to the effect of static electricity (just like human hair the day after shampooing). This means that your dog's coat, which normally keeps heat in (insulation) and keeps water out (waterproofing), can't perform these important functions. Without skin oils, the new generation of flea and tick products cannot function. These drugs, which are applied to the skin between the shoulder blades, need oils in the skin to enable them to spread over your pet's body and prevent those nasties. What's more, it is possible to make healthy skin look sick through over-bathing. So no matter how much you might want to, don't over-bathe your dog. Oils add the all-important shine and lustre to your dog's coat.

ADDING LUSTRE

To add some extra shine to your pet's coat add fish oils (containing omega-3) to their food. Premium pet foods now contain fish oils, but you can also get them from your vet. Within a few weeks, you'll notice that your pet's coat takes on a brilliant lustre. This is an example of an oil that is good for your pet. Fish oils also help the immune system, skin and heart.

The best method

Bath time always seems to be far more difficult than it should be. If kids can learn to have fun in a bath, then so can your dog. Understanding why it can become such a traumatic experience for owner and animal, may help to make it a whole lot more pleasant. The basic issue with washing your dog is that it combines a number of incidents that produce fear. Just think about it: the sound of the hose, the sight of the same bathtub, the feeling of the water being too cold or too hot or with high pressure, the smell of detergents, the inability to flee as well as the immersion in the water bringing out fears of water and drowning. These elements are always going to make it hard to convince your dog that a bath is a good idea and maybe even fun.

The key to making the whole process a success is to remember that it's all a foreign experience and to minimise as many of the negative, fear-producing factors (sights, sounds and smells) as possible. Starting from a young age will allow your pup to get used to the experience.

I reckon the quickest and easiest way is to:

1 Fill a bucket with lukewarm water and add a few squirts of dog shampoo (low perfume and soap-free). Mix the shampoo and water together well.

2 Take your dog into an enclosed area (shower recess or bathroom is ideal). Once there, reward him/her with some liver treats or dog biscuits and give plenty of reassurance and pats. Even bring in some favourite toys.

3 Using a large, soft sponge, gently transfer the shampoo mix onto the dogs coat and work it into a lather. Add more of the shampoo mix with the sponge, ensuring the foam penetrates right down to the skin all across the dog. Give special attention to the muzzle, between the legs and around the rear end. These tend to be the smelliest areas. Give reassurance and pats.

Shake it! The first step to a dry coat.

What dog doesn't like an all-over 'body pat'?

4 Using either a hand-held shower head, or another fresh bucket of lukewarm water, rinse out the shampoo from the highest points on the dog to the lowest points. Talk to your dog constantly through this process and let them know that they're not alone. If your dog begins to fret then stop and have a break. You should only resume when they seem at ease. Food rewards will help here.

5 Once fully rinsed, use a towel to dry them off. This must feel like one gigantic all-over body pat, so dogs usually like this part. If your dog still isn't dry, then allow them to dry off in the shower recess or in the sun. Never leave a wet dog in the cold or wind as they will freeze. A thick coat will take longer than you think to dry. Using a fan heater (on low power) may help.

The emphasis is always on having fun. If your dog isn't having fun then slow down and wait until they are more comfortable. Food rewards and toys are always great party starters.

TIP

Pay special attention to drying out the ear-canals, especially on dogs with long, floppy ears. Water trapped in ears is one of the main contributors to painful and smelly ear infections.

What shampoo should I use?

This is really important: never use human shampoo. I have seen dogs that have had their skin burned by their owners mistakenly using human shampoo. The reason is that human and dog skin are just so different. We know that dogs' skin is thinner and more fragile, but it also has a totally different pH level as well. The pH measures the acidity (and alkalinity) of substances — the lower the pH, the more acidic. Human skin and human shampoo are a lot more acidic (pH around 5) than dogs' skin and shampoo (pH around 7). In fact, human shampoo is around 100 times more acidic than dogs' skin or dogs' shampoo. So using human shampoo on dogs means that it can actually burn their skin like acid. On a dog, human shampoo will:

- Dissolve and wash away all of the important skin and coat oils.
- Dry the skin and make it itchy and red. It is then more likely to get infected by bacteria.
- Burn the thin and weak outer layers of the skin.

Puppy skin is even more fragile and prone to drying out. So ensure you take extra-special care when bathing and even water down the shampoo so it's not too harsh on their skin.

I would recommend that you always use soap-free dog shampoos. They are pH balanced, meaning they are just right for dogs' skin. Being soap-free, they do not remove oils but will dislodge the dirt and odour. Many now contain conditioners as well.

GROOMING

When grooming is mentioned, the first thought is often of permed, perfumed and manicured creatures, adorned with ribbon bows, prancing their way into salons and parlours to demand a cut and blow dry — and that's only the owners. So let's talk about the real world of pet grooming.

Grooming really covers the whole spectrum of pet care from a simple brush down, right through to a complex and extravagant poodle trim. The amount of time, effort and cost involved really is a major consideration when choosing a pet.

Often, the grooming of an animal into a certain style has evolved that way for a reason. Taking into account its coat type or the animal's function (such as hunting), it may be the most practical way to keep the coat clean and free of tangles. So despite all the hype surrounding hairdos, there is a practical side to it all. The main reasons why pets are groomed are to:

- Make the animal look acceptable to you and other people.
- Reduce the amount of hair shed onto you, the floor and furniture.
- Reduce the amount of hair ingested, which may then cause fur balls (in cats and rabbits).
- Reduce the chance of knots forming. These cause significant pain and skin damage to the pet. They also look unsightly.

NOT GROOMING?

If your cat looks a little rough around the edges it could be that they have stopped grooming themselves. Not grooming is a common sign of illness, and in older cats a sign of arthritis or joint pain. So a bad hairstyle may be more serious than first thought.

There really isn't one animal that doesn't benefit from grooming of some sort, even if it is just a quick brush to remove dead hair and skin cells.

Grooming tips

My biggest tips for grooming are:

- Start brushing and cleaning around your pet's ears and eyes from a young age — it will allow them to become comfortable with the process that may be a common occurrence in later life.
- Regular brushing, although time consuming, prevents painful and potentially expensive (to remove) knots from forming.
- Get your pet used to having its nails trimmed from a young age. Your vet or your groomer can show you how. It means your pet won't be too precious about it later on in life. Having the hair trimmed between the toes is also recommended.
- It's important that all long-haired and floppy-eared dogs have their ear hair managed. Excess hair in this area allows moisture and dirt to be trapped in the ear canal and make ear infections more likely. So it's a matter of either keeping the ear canals meticulously clean, or just having the hair plucked right out of there.
- Many people like to clip their long-haired dogs and cats as a way of helping them to handle the summer heat. This is a great idea and is also handy for those dogs with skin conditions. I reckon the real benefit lies in the fact that ticks and fleas are more easily detected too.
- Keep the hair trimmed short and brushed away from the eyes of dogs. This is especially important in those pets with exposed eyes, such as shih tzus, malteses, bichon frises and poodles of all sizes.
- When brushing your pet, use the time to check for signs of fleas, ticks or skin diseases (such as pimples, rashes, welts, greasy skin or flaky skin).

Tear staining is a common problem if you're small, white and fluffy.

Tear staining

Tear stains are unsightly brown marks that appear just below the inner corner of some pets' eyes. There are a few possible reasons for this:

- The tear ducts (which allow tears to flow from the eyes to the nostrils) are blocked, which causes a build-up and then an overflow of tears.
- There is infection in the eyes (conjunctivitis).
- There is an allergy affecting the eyes (hay fever).

Tear staining is not serious — it just looks that way. Your vet can establish the cause and help keep the tears to a minimum. You can remove the tear stains by either using a soft cloth soaked in salty water, or a 'tear-stain remover' (a specially designed liquid) and wiping away from the eyes.

Grooming for dogs

Grooming for dogs can be a style choice or a matter of practicality. Whatever the reason, most dogs love a good brush. It stimulates blood flow to the skin, removes dirt and dead skin cells as well as removing any hair that's being shed. Be sure to keep your eyes open for any scurrying fleas (especially around the base of the tail and between the legs) or telltale flea dirt (red-brown specks) that may be hiding deep within the coat.

Short-coated dogs

These breeds (boxers, bull terriers, staffies, jack russells, kelpies, and so on) require a low level of grooming. They need less attention than other dogs and usually no professional help is required. Use a stiff brush that shifts loose hair and dead skin cells at least once a week. A glove brush can also make the task a lot easier. Even though they require far less grooming than longer-haired breeds, they will shed a large amount of hair.

Rough- or wire-coated dogs

These breeds (West Highland terriers, airedales, and so on) require a low level of grooming. Rather than constant shedding, these coats tend to be lost in 'waves'. 'Mats' rather than knots are the biggest concern in this coat type. A daily brush is ideal. A stiff brush is the main piece of equipment required, but a comb will also help. Professional help is occasionally required.

Silky-coated dogs

These breeds (cocker spaniels, Irish setters, pekingese, and so on) require a medium level of grooming. Longer strands of hair are shed but not as frequently as in the short-coated dogs. A daily brush is beneficial. Use a stiff brush and a comb. Asking a dog groomer for a hand with these guys isn't out of the question.

Long-coated dogs

These breeds (poodles of all sizes, afghan hounds, old english sheepdogs, and so on) require a high level of grooming. Grooming is a big consideration — an alternative may be to have the coat clipped short regularly if this suits, although this may negate the whole attraction of having one of these dogs. Daily brushing is essential — a long comb is vital along with a firm brushing. A monthly visit to a professional groomer is almost essential. Clipping is commonly required. A regular ear clean or plucking of ear hair is one of the most important aspects of grooming in these breeds (especially poodles).

DID YOU KNOW?

Even camels need regular brushing. It's especially important after winter when their thick, wiry winter coats must be shed to enable them to manage the approaching hot summer months. Camel owners need to brush them with thick wiry brushes to shift the coat and have large scratching posts nearby which helps the camel to rub away excess hair.

Short-haired dogs like Rosie have a low-maintenance go-anywhere haircut that doesn't change with the seasons.

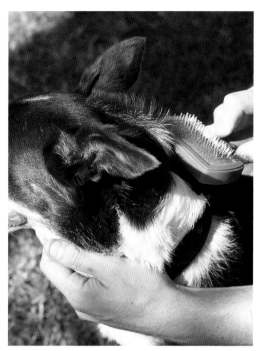

Some are simply born with style. No brush could ever hope to move that mohawk.

Cats are great self-stylists. However, some extra help wouldn't go astray.

FUR BALLS

Fur balls occur when hair swallowed during grooming forms clumps in the stomach. These are then regurgitated. To prevent them, brush your cat regularly and use a 'fur ball remover'. This is a laxative gel that you feed your cat to enable them to digest the hair, rather than have to bring it back up. Some specially-designed cat foods now help to prevent fur balls.

Grooming for cats

Cats certainly consider themselves their own stylist. In fact, most healthy cats are devoted self-groomers. But no matter how much they might object to it, extra help is required by long-haired and semi long-haired cats. However, even short-haired cats and 'hairless' cats can do with more than just the standard technique of tongue, paws and claws.

Short-haired cats

These breeds (burmese, siamese, russian blue, and so on) require a low level of grooming. Their self-grooming is usually sufficient, however, a quick going-over with a rubber-bristled brush will help to remove any dead hair and dandruff. If fur balls or excess shedding are a problem, then daily brushing will be beneficial. This also applies to older cats with arthritis, that may have trouble grooming their whole body. An occasional ear clean and wipe around the eyes will help the cat look its best. A final wipe over with a chamois or velvet glove will give a 'showroom' shine to their coat.

Long-haired cats

These breeds (persian, birman, ragdoll, and so on) require a high level of grooming. Regular daily brushing (with a wide-toothed metal comb) is the only way to prevent knotting of a long-haired coat. Knots, especially in the underarm and groin area, are a real problem as they tug on the skin and make moving freely a painful and near-impossible task. If knots do form, try teasing them out with your fingers. Then try a fine comb, holding the knot at its base so you are not tugging on the skin. If all of these measures are unsuccessful then speak with a professional groomer. The only humane and practical solution may be to shave the cat short, which may even require sedation. Getting the nails trimmed short at the same time

might just save you when the cat wants to let out some anger over its new look. Regular, short clips are often the only realistic and practical way to care for these cats. Along with fur ball removing supplements, short clips help to keep these cats fur ball free. Many of my clients with long-haired cats have them clipped regularly as a way of minimising the grooming required. It is often the only realistic way to care for these cats.

Hairless cats

Living your life as a nude (sphinx, rex, and so on) doesn't mean no grooming. In fact it's the opposite, as having no clothes on should (and does) attract more attention. Instead of brushing, they need frequent 'sponging' with a damp cloth. It sounds strange, but not having a thick hair coat means that their skin is exposed. If accumulated oils and dirt are not sponged off, then this naked animal will leave greasy marks on you and on the furniture, as well as predisposing them to skin infections.

Short-haired cats, like this Russian blue, appreciate some help to remove dead hair.

For long-haired cats, like this ragdoll, daily brushing is the key to avoiding knots.

FEEDING

Aside from a hairstyle that never looks under control, I reckon there is one big thing I have in common with dogs. It's that dinner is definitely the highlight of the day. The day's work is done — which means there is nothing more to do than put the feet (or paws) up and tuck into something that makes it all worthwhile.

But even though the desire to eat is such a simple one, it's amazing how complicated feeding a pet can be made. I often see new pet owners arrive home from a breeder with feeding instructions that make the recipe for a five-course organic, low gluten, low GI, hormone free, hypoallergenic meal seem pretty simple in comparison. There will be different types of meats, vegetables (mashed and boiled), milk, butter, calcium supplements, fibre additives, salt, rice, pasta, herbs, spices and whatever else is seen as important. My approach has always been 'Why complicate something that can be very simple?'. This is especially important in our new fast-paced world where we have trouble finding the time to cook ourselves a meal, let alone one for our pets.

The great thing is that most of the hard work has been done for you by premium pet food manufacturers. These select few, high-quality companies, spend millions of dollars each year finding out exactly what your pets want and most importantly, need (ask your vet for their recommendations). Their exact requirements for protein, carbohydrates, fats, vitamins and minerals, are calculated and precisely incorporated into the foods. The certainty in meeting the nutritional requirements of your pet makes this way of feeding far superior to the hit and miss affair of home-cooked meals. All the effort in attempting to source often obscure ingredients is also eliminated. But most importantly for your little buddy, the taste of the food receives just as much attention as the quality of the ingredients. The reason for this is obvious, if your pet won't eat the food, then how are they going to benefit from what's actually in it?

All you need to do is consider what type and how much food to give, and how often to feed.

What food?

Dogs and cats are carnivores, which means they need a high level of meat in their diet to provide them with most of the nutrients they need. Carbohydrates for extra energy, fats, vitamins and minerals are also crucial if you want a happy and healthy pet. But the issue is really how you can give your pet these ingredients in the best possible way. Not only so that they are given them at every meal, but also so they are able to digest and absorb them fully while gaining as much benefit from their meal as possible.

Try to use a complete dry food. These are the type recommended by vets and sold from vet clinics and some pet stores and suppliers. They are of a consistent high quality. Also, the additional benefits these foods provide for the teeth, skin and coat, as well as producing less waste, aren't found in home-cooked or supermarket products. Even though complete dry foods seem more expensive than other dry foods, they are more concentrated, meaning you will feed less and the food will last longer. Also, they tend to be more digestible so that less food is wasted. Canned foods are around 80 per cent water, so your pet will need to eat a lot more canned food than dry food to get all the energy they require.

Use a food that is suited to their age and size. Some points to consider:

- Puppy / kitten foods are higher in protein, calcium and energy.
- Growth diets enable pets (especially dogs, where it is crucial) to grow at a controlled rate — and not too quickly.
- Adult pet foods contain a stable level of essential nutrients, as your pet needs less energy as it is no longer growing. Adult foods are split into small, medium and large breed formulations.
- Senior diets contain more fibre, for digestion, antioxidants, to boost the immune system, and joint supplements to help arthritis.
- Prescription diets are designed to help pets manage a particular disease by making alterations in what they eat.

Food for cats

True to their renowned self-centred character, cats have special food requirements. They need high levels of protein and some nutrients (vitamin A and taurine) only found in meat-based diets like chicken, beef and lamb. That's why a cat can actually go blind through only being fed fish, rather than a balanced diet. You should expose your cat to as many different food types and flavours as possible in the first 6 months of life. If our feline friends haven't been exposed to a particular type of food as a kitten, then it's near impossible to get them to eat it as an adult. So when they need to eat a type of food for a medical reason, unless they've seen it before, you've got little hope.

How often?

This varies with age. I would recommend:

- at 6–12 weeks: 4 times a day
- at 12–24 weeks: 3 times a day
- at 24 weeks onwards: 2 times a day.

This can drop to once a day at 12 months. After 12 months of age, there is much debate over what is better for your pets. The best way to decide is to look at what is important for you and your pet.

Once a day

This frequency of feeding is recommended for:

- Pets that can become too needy for food. Being fed at a regular time once a day, lessens their dependence on you. This pattern makes begging and whining for food less likely.
- People that are busy and may not routinely be able to feed twice a day.
- Pets that receive large bones or treats to chew on during the day.

If feeding once a day, feed at night. This stops hungry dogs and cats from barking or meowing for food, and makes them less inclined to wander in search of a meal. Like us, a good meal is best followed by a good sleep.

Twice a day

This frequency of feeding is recommended for:

- Pets that are prone to obesity. Research shows that the acts of eating and digesting burn large amounts of energy. So oddly, eating often can help lose weight provided the same total daily amount is given, but in two separate feeds.
- Pets that are prone to eating large amounts too quickly.
- Very small dogs or cats. Generally, the smaller the animal, the higher the metabolic rate.

How much to serve?

The phrase 'You can never have too much' certainly doesn't apply to our pets. But sadly, the 'all you can eat' buffet is an all too frequently encountered situation. Remember that most pets are never satisfied, no matter how much you give them, so don't fall for the old sad eyes and whining trick. It's important to reinforce that what you give them is all they're going to get, no matter how much they beg, borrow or try to steal.

This is another situation where using a complete pet food takes away the 'hit and miss' element of deciding 'how much' to feed. Because these meals are of a reliable and exact level of energy, you are able to know precisely how much is required to keep your pet at an ideal weight. Next time you're shopping, check out the feeding guides on the back of the packaging. Quite simply, they will show you the exact amount that your pet should have. I just think that this is so much easier than trying to measure out handfuls of meat while trying to guess such things as whether the meat is fattier than last time, meaning there should be less of it.

Obviously if you are in any doubt at all, then speak to your vet and they will explain how much you need. The new age of complete and premium pet food takes a number of factors into account when determining how much your pet will need. Like us, different animals require different amounts of food to keep at a certain weight. When you calculate exactly how much you need to feed, that figure is based on the average amount required. But your pet's lifestyle and metabolic rate might make that too much or too little for their needs. So check them regularly to see if they are too fat or too thin and adjust accordingly.

Your pet's meal size is influenced by their age, lifestyle and breed.

The meal size changes with age

Growing animals need more than fully grown animals of the same size. Adult animals need comparatively less, as they no longer need energy for growth. Elderly animals are prone to becoming overweight, so may require fewer calories but higher levels of fibre to help aid digestion. All these factors should be taken into account when feeding these pets.

The meal size changes with lifestyle

Less active pets (that live inside or don't get exercise) should eat less. Highly active pets (those exercised a couple of times a day) can be fed more, provided they don't pack on weight. Some dogs gain weight no matter how often they exercise.

The meal size changes with breed

Those dog breeds that will be over 25 kg (55 lb) when adults should be fed a specially formulated diet while they are growing. This is called a large-breed growth diet, and is designed for dogs the size of labradors, golden retrievers, great danes, rottweilers, dalmatians and standard poodles. These animals will be fed less than their size suggests they need. This is a deliberate way of slowing their growth and development of bones and joints, which can help to avoid problems like hip dysplasia, OCD (*Osteochondritis dissecans*, a joint cartilage abnormality), and the early onset of arthritis. You should never supplement their diet with calcium or energy-producing additives. If your breeder tells you to add anything to your pet's food, you should first ask your local vet for their approval.

Some breeds can't help but look chubby! If you're confused, simply ask your vet for their opinion.

Is my pet is too fat?

It's all about the ribs. If you can see the ribs when you look at your pet, then it's too thin. If you can't feel each rib when you run your fingers along their chest (it should feel like a sheet of corrugated iron), then they're too fat. So the ribs should be felt, but not seen. In cats, excess fat is also stored in the folds of skin around the belly. It's their form of the good old 'beer belly' and it's a sign that they are eating too much.

Off the menu

Why is it that pets always seem to want what we're eating? While our food is usually good for us, it can be a real problem for our little mates. The following are a few foods to keep off the menu.

Chocolate

Pets love the taste almost as much as we do, but chocolate is toxic and will cause vomiting, diarrhoea and restlessness which can progress to seizures, heart failure and even death. A standard 250 g (9 oz) chocolate block can be enough to kill a small dog. Dark chocolate is more toxic than milk and white varieties.

Onions

A must at every barbecue, but keep them off limits to Fido. They will cause a serious anaemia (lack of red blood cells) in dogs if eaten in excess.

Bones

Cooked bones (especially lamb chop bones) are a disaster for all pets. Ensure no meat or discarded bones are left lying around after a barbecue. A few crafty canines deft in the art of stealing from plates get themselves in trouble every year.

Nuts

Nuts are high in fat and will cause gut upsets and even liver and pancreas problems if eaten. Macadamia nuts are the most toxic of all.

Spicy foods

Our foods are generally more spicy and rich than our pets are used to digesting. Even though they may enjoy the taste more than their usual food, it's the usual story of what tastes good isn't necessarily the best for you. So feed them what they're meant to eat, not what they want to eat.

Treats and bones

Treats are a great way of showing how much you care about your pet and they also help with training. Just remember why they are so popular — they are often high in fat and salt, which makes them taste great. So, if you're giving your pets treats, then make sure they are low in fat (biscuits or kibble are often better than meaty chews) and ensure you feed them a little less for dinner — otherwise that treat will go straight to the hips.

Bones do make up an important part of a dog's or cat's diet. They're a handy way of keeping their teeth clean — and your pet will derive a great deal of pleasure out of chewing them. But they can be dangerous. Only ever feed raw bones. Cooked bones can splinter into sharp pieces when they are chewed, which may cause injury to the mouth and throat, and can cause potentially fatal damage to the stomach and intestines. Raw chicken wings (for dogs and cats) are a good way to start. Bigger dogs can progress onto large leg bones once fully grown.

Try starting your dog or cat on bones at around 12 weeks of age. Give them a small piece of chicken wing and supervise any early encounters.

Dealing with common dining complaints

Being overly picky

At some stage during your pet's life, they will try this one on you. Turning their nose up at a particular type of food when they are quite clearly hungry is a strategy designed to improve the meal in front of them. If you are feeding a high-quality food and your pet seems well otherwise, then you must be firm and not give in by replacing it with something tastier. Otherwise, before you know it, you'll be serving up a medium-rare choice cut steak in béarnaise sauce. If you give in once, then they will always try it on.

If your pet starts to be picky, then leave the food where it is. If you are in a hot climate then you can remove the food but only ever replace it with the same type. Pets are highly instinctive animals and won't let themselves starve. Speak to your vet if their hunger strike goes past 2 days or if they show any signs of illness.

'I DIDN'T TOUCH IT' HALL OF FAME

In much the same way as a salt-encrusted old fisherman will reminisce about 'the one that got away', the following animals have nothing but the memories (and sometimes the scars) of 'the one that got *in the way*'.

Flicstix the beagle ate her way through 30 contraceptive pills and lived to tell the tale. Although she is now a little more prone to mood swings...

Alexis the samoyed 'suction unit' ate her way through 3 pairs of socks, a teddy bear leg and 2 G-strings, for a total of 6 exploratory surgeries.

Goda the blue heeler x really made a name for himself when, as his owners were making mango chutney, he intercepted a mango stone on its way to the bin. A thousand dollars and a good scar later, the mango chutney now bears his name.

Aria 'Hoover' Hunt, in her short life span, has managed to consume stones, 3 teddy bear eyes, 4 legs and the entire foam contents of a mattress — and she actually has a food allergy.

Rommel Rex ate his way through 4 whole corn cobs before he was all cobbed out. They were all removed from his insides and then removed from his sight for fear of him regaining his hunger.

Max Boyd ate an entire puffer fish. For a dog in the new millennium, it was as close as he ever got to the psychedelic 60s. Hallucinations and tremors disappeared after a day on an intravenous drip.

Pluto Keeling's medical condition didn't stop him from consuming paint and a block of blue cheese. He then tried to increase his diminishing value by tucking into a collection of precious stones that were never seen again.

Goda, founder (and producer) of the famous mango chutney.

Gaining weight despite feeding the right amount

Most likely, your pet's metabolism is such that the 'right' amount of food is actually too much for their requirements. So tailor the amount to what they need. Try dropping the total amount by 25 per cent and seeing if the weight has changed in one month. Also, try a bit more exercise and watch the number of treats that are passing their lips. Never dismiss the possibility that your pet could be enjoying the benefits of befriending a neighbour for food.

Losing weight despite feeding the right amount

Firstly check that the amount you are feeding is correct. Then look more closely at what is going on. Could another animal be stealing food? Could they have worms? Losing weight can be a significant sign of illness. Talk to your vet about the problem.

THE TOP FIVE FAVOURITE PET JUNK 'FOODS'

String How long is a piece of string? Well just ask a vet. That's because cats and dogs find this fun to play with and often can't resist swallowing it. It will cause a blockage in the gut that usually requires surgery.

Socks and underwear To a pet, these smell great and, well, taste great too. It's an extra incentive to stop leaving smelly socks around. And in terms of underwear, I reckon I've seen more G-strings come out of dogs than come out of a lingerie store.

Parts of toys and teddy bears Toys are often brightly coloured and have very chewable pieces. Teddy bears with any missing eyes, legs or other parts should arouse suspicion.

Food wrappers Sure it doesn't quite have the same texture as the food it once contained, but it still has some of the taste. Therein lies the problem. They are easily found if left lying around.

Bones Most people know you should never feed cooked bones. However, cooked bones may be snatched off a barbecue or out of bins when owners aren't looking. Being cooked, they may shatter into sharp pieces when chewed and won't be digested in the stomach. An expensive surgery is often the result.

Vomiting up dinner

Rather than being a reflection on your choice of food for them, there is always a reason why a pet will vomit. However, this may or may not be a serious problem (unless it's on the carpet — when it's always serious). The important thing here is how soon after eating it occurs and whether the food looks digested or not.

If the vomiting occurs soon after eating and the food remains undigested, then it's most likely due to the animal eating too much and/or eating too quickly. This is common in anxious animals that eat quickly to ensure that no other animal is able to get to their food. It is also seen in households that have more than one pet, as there is competition for food. And, of course, in those pets that are vacuum cleaners — those that 'inhale' their food. This is not a major concern. Try feeding smaller meals, while still feeding the same total amount in a day, and separate animals in multi-pet households. If this doesn't help, then speak to your vet.

If vomiting occurs sometime after eating and the food is partly digested, then this is most likely due to a gut upset or digestive problem. This is a more serious problem and may require a vet's attention. Ensure you remove their food for at least 12–24 hours. If the digestive tract isn't ready for food, then they will only vomit if fed again. Take away their water for at least 4 hours, as a big drink will only cause another vomit, then only allow them small drinks every hour for the next 8–20 hours.

Diarrhoea

The most common cause of diarrhoea in young animals is eating too much. Suspect overeating as the cause of diarrhoea in those pets that have a good appetite, seem happy and have been wormed. The reason is that their small stomach can't handle all that food, so much of it goes through too quickly without being digested properly.

You may like to try feeding a little bit less; try decreasing the total amount by 25 per cent. If signs persist, or the animal appears unwell, then speak to your vet. Gut upsets, viruses, stomach bugs or worms are among the causes of more serious diarrhoea in puppies. Diarrhoea in an unvaccinated puppy should always be regarded as serious.

Ordering the wrong meal

This includes all those highly appealing activities like scavenging through the garbage, chewing plants and toys and even (your favourite and mine) eating poo. This is really pets just being pets. Most of this type of behaviour is borne out of being inquisitive, adventurous, or even bored. It is rare for an animal that is being fed a proper diet to need to derive nutrients through eating these 'added extras'. In order to put an end to this sort of behaviour, you must make it clear that this behaviour is not on. You must catch them in the act, say a firm 'no' and remove them from the scene of the crime and into another area. If there seems to be a fascination with a particular object then try spraying it with citronella oil, as this is a strong deterrent for pets. A dash of hot Tabasco sauce may also help deter a pup from seeing poo as a viable source of food in the future. You could even inject it into the poo for a hidden surprise.

An occasional poo-eater is actually displaying symptoms of being deficient in a digestive enzyme, which they're trying to extract from the faeces. Feeding these pets some boiled pumpkin may help to restore the enzyme and ease their poo-eating problem.

MAKING YOUR HOUSE
A SAFE-HOUSE

A new pet faces many hurdles in their first few months of life. After all, they are small, vulnerable and have to solve a multitude of mysteries. Like 'when will I be fed?', and 'where do I go to the toilet?'. There is also the challenge of identifying whose bed can and can't be slept on, and who is a sucker for feeding from the table. With all these things to learn, there is one question that can't be done without — what is safe to play with, chew and eat?

Plants

Plants can often be an unforeseen danger to our pets. Having some greenery in the garden and the house is a great way of adding life to these areas. It certainly shouldn't endanger your pets, and it won't, providing you are smart about what plants you have and where you put them. Never ignore the fact that an inquisitive pet (especially an agile kitten or a playful puppy) can, and probably will, access almost all parts of the garden and house if allowed. And that's when the trouble can start. But I know what you're thinking — you have a tough time as it is getting your pup or kitten to eat their special 'formulated diets', it's never going to decide that a salad is the way to go. However, never discount the fact that even though your pet may not be renowned as a salad eater, the curious mind and playful desires of young animals often override any reservations they might have had over the taste of the plant.

As a vet, I see a few classic situations where pets get themselves into trouble:

- Cut flowers and floral displays. For an animal new to this world, nothing arouses more interest than a bright, decorative and extravagant bunch of flowers. Just think about it; they appeal to almost all the senses. So a closer look is almost compulsory. And even though your pet is in the relative safety of your house, cut flowers are often from some of our most toxic plants.

- Dogs that chase sticks. Dogs of all ages that are mad over chasing (and then chewing) sticks should be closely supervised. A stick is not just a stick when it could be a piece of toxic plant in your dog's mouth. To make matters worse, the thrill of the game will often override any unpleasant taste coming from the wood.

- Puppies and kittens that are teething. The teething stage (8 weeks–6 months) is when the urge to chew anything and everything takes over. With this in mind, it's not hard to see why more poisonings and intoxications occur at this age than at any other.

Keep a close watch on teething puppies.

PLANTS TO WATCH

If you want to play it 100 per cent safe, consider every plant as a potential danger, and try to discourage a pet from chewing, let alone eating, even the smallest amount of greenery. The following are listed as major dangers:

- Lilies. Curiosity can certainly kill the cat! Lilies are a major killer of cats (especially kittens). So much so that you should never have any lilies in flower arrangements, or even growing in the garden if you own a cat. All parts of the plant are toxic. Even the simple act of munching on a tiny leaf or petal can cause kidney failure and death. If you suspect your cat has eaten lilies, then get it to the vet as soon as possible. In dogs, eating lilies will cause a gut upset, but few other signs.

- Other bulbs, such as daffodils, tulips and jonquils. While the flowers and stems aren't as toxic as the lily family of plants, I would still keep these plants off limits. Daffodils can cause poisonings, but it's really the bulbs themselves that are the main concern. The toxin within the bulbs (an alkaloid) can be released if a puppy or kitten mistakes the round bulb for a ball to play with and chew.

- Yesterday, Today, Tomorrow (Brunfelsia australis). Really nasty if eaten as it can cause convulsions and symptoms similar to strychnine poisoning.

- Cotoneaster glaucophyllus. Eating the fruits of this plant can cause paralysis.

- Savin (Juniperus sabina). All parts of this plant are toxic and must be avoided.

- Blue–green algae. Affects ponds and stagnant water in summer. Never allow pets to drink from these places, as the results can be fatal.

- Rhubarb. The leaves on these plants are toxic and should never be fed to chickens or other birds.
- Oleander. All parts are highly toxic.
- Macadamia nuts. These nuts can be toxic if ingested by pets.
- Azaleas. The leaves are toxic.
- Poinsettia. The leaves are toxic.
- Rhododendrons. The leaves are toxic.
- Apricot kernels. Can be poisonous if chewed.

Many plants can cause an allergy and different pets will be allergic to different plants. However, Wandering Jew (Tradescantia fluminensis) is an extremely common cause of allergies. Pets, and especially dogs, that walk or lie on the plant, inevitably come in contact with the sap which sticks to the skin and causes a red, itchy rash.

Small object = big problem

And you thought having a pet was easier than having a child! When it comes to toys and small, fascinating objects around the home, the same rules apply. After all, they get around the house on much the same level. But don't forget that some pets can jump too. Anything that can be chewed and swallowed represents a potential hazard.

Choking and gut obstructions are the main worries, so if you see any difficulty breathing or swallowing, vomiting and signs of discomfort, then be alarmed, especially if there are things missing from around the home. The time of teething (2-6 months) is the main danger time.

TIP

To give a tablet the sneaky way, grind it into a fine powder between two spoons. Mix the powder with a dollop of butter and honey to make a paste. Then smear it in the sides of their gums, or let them lick it up themselves.

So hot right now

Heaters and fireplaces are designed to keep us comfortable, but can spell danger for our pets if they don't keep their distance. People I talk to are often mystified as to how and why their pets insist on lying so close to heaters. The thick fur of a pet will mean they remain unaware that the outer layers of their hair are at scorching temperatures. Singeing of the hair and burns to the skin can and do result. Lying too close to fireplaces also increases the risk of burns from hot coals that spit out from fires. It's one example of when you shouldn't let sleeping dogs lie.

If you want to make sure that your pet isn't getting too hot under the collar, then try this. Tape a strip-type thermometer to your pet's collar and see exactly what temperature the outer layers of fur are reaching. Anything over 35°C (95°F) and they're too hot.

And as for cooling fans, you should always keep these covered and out of reach of pets. The blades spin so fast that your pet is unlikely to know that it's even there. This is especially important for the safety of birds.

Sparking an interest

Power cords snaking across a room can make an attractive play toy for a pet, however, the truth of what they actually are can come as a shock. Unfortunately, I do see a number of pets every year that have chewed into or through power cords. Where possible, conceal the cords under carpets or protective mats and use circuit breakers in the fuse box for added protection. Birds (especially cockatoos) and rabbits are known cord-chewing culprits.

Washing machines and clothes driers are fascinating for your average pet. All the smells, sounds and movement can combine to make a look inside almost irresistible. Ensure you keep lids and doors closed to prevent unwanted visitors.

Hot stove tops are often a major attraction because of the smells that magically waft from them. Never leave them unattended.

Hard pill to swallow

Your vet is the only person that should be prescribing medications to your pet. Although many people have their own virtual pharmacy of tablets and syrups lurking in a cupboard, many of these human remedies can be harmful or even fatal to a pet. To make matters worse, the most commonly used human drugs (like paracetamol and aspirin) are some of the most toxic to pets, especially cats. However, you will be fine provided you never give a pet anything that isn't specifically designed for them.

It's one of the ironies of owning a pet that getting an animal to swallow a tablet is near impossible, while pets getting stuck into tablets of their own accord is quite common. Over the last few years, a lot of work has been put into making pet medications more palatable for dogs and cats to swallow. Tasty tablets combined with fun-to-chew packaging and foil makes them a real hit with an inquisitive pet. Always keep all medications in high, closed cupboards to avoid your pet having an overdose. The same goes for human medications, which are often sugar-coated or in easy-to-digest liquid form.

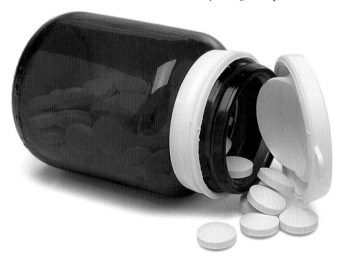

Purring engines

In winter, pets are attracted to the warmth of car engines and cats may even get up into the engine compartment from underneath. When the car is started, a cat risks serious injury from the moving fan belt or fan blades. In summer, pets will often lie under parked cars to keep out of the hot sun. So, like a pilot, conduct a pre-flight check before you drive off, and check for any unwanted passengers or obstacles.

Chemicals and poisons

A poison or 'bait' (such as snail and rat baits) should be considered toxic for all animals and not just the intended snail or rat. Remember that these products are designed to be attractive to eat, as that is the way they attract their victims in the first place. Frustratingly, many manufacturers claim that they actually repel or are unattractive to pets. This is simply not the case, so never take the chance. Snail and rat baits should only ever be used where you are sure your pet is unable to access them and preferably not at all, especially when young and curious animals are around. If you have any suspicion that these products have been eaten, then early treatment by a vet delivers the best results. Never sit back and wait for signs to show up, as this is usually too late.

Fortunately most harmful chemicals have putrid tastes that keep pets away. However, never discount the effect of an inquisitive and curious mind. Along with snail and rat baits, some other commonly found chemicals can cause severe illness in pets. In cold areas, antifreeze for cars can cause problems for pets due to its sweet taste. It is highly toxic and can kill animals through kidney failure. Lead paint (common in older houses) can also attract a bored or inquisitive animal, especially if it is flaking.

You might have noticed that in pets, there's not much that a good lick can't fix. They see a good lick as their answer to a bath or even a bandage. However, it can also get them into trouble. Pets that come into contact with chemicals by simply walking through them or having them spilt on their fur, will do what comes naturally; lick themselves clean, even if the taste isn't one to rave about. You must consider that any substance that touches their fur will probably end up in their mouth. Human antiseptics that are applied to wounds should never be used without prior approval from a vet. Oil, turpentine or paints can easily be walked or lain in, which is not a massive problem until the natural licking action brings it to the mouth where they cause severe and serious burns to the mouth and throat.

Be quick to clean up any chemical spills and keep pets out of garages and work sheds. If you do see a substance on the fur of a pet, then be quick to clean the coat with an animal-safe shampoo. Problems are caused, however, when a chemical has a pleasant taste. Generally anything that smells pleasant to you will pose a risk.

TIP
In winter, a quick honk on the horn or a bang on the hood of the car may provide enough warning for a cat to make a quick getaway.

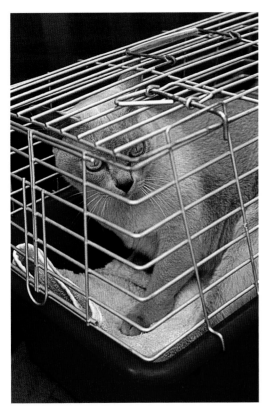

A cat basket makes a safe travel option.

HOLIDAYS AND TRAVELLING

If you've been working like a dog and you need a holiday, the worry of what to do with a pet can take the gloss off a well-earned break. Nowadays though, there are so many options, it's often hard to tell who gets the better holiday deal.

There are a couple of careful considerations to make before you take your pet away.

The type of pet

Dogs are the best travellers, while cats are prone to becoming anxious. Cats like their own space and their own smells and if stressed are at risk of running away. Bear in mind that many animals that are considered pets in one part of Australia may be considered pests in another and may be illegal to own. Be especially careful with rabbits and ferrets.

The health of your pet

The stress of travelling, the change in environment and routine, and the increased activity on holidays will put extra strain on your pet if they are not already feeling 100 per cent. Pets (and sometimes parents) in need of peace and quiet are often not suited to family holidays.

How will you get there? How long will it take?

Some pets travel poorly no matter whether they are flying first class aboard a luxury jet or on the back seat of the car. These pets are typically the most anxious and have trouble adjusting to the new surrounds that a holiday brings anyway. If your pet is okay with short trips by car to the local vet, then chances are that a drive to a holiday spot will be fine. If you are in any doubt then take them on a test-run well before you plan to travel. You are far better off knowing that they are a poor traveller or get carsick easily than discovering this first hand when you are halfway to the holiday destination. Travelling at night can often make a nervous traveller more relaxed. Ensure that small dogs and cats have a travelling case (with plenty of ventilation) and large dogs have a harness enabling them to be strapped in and safe in the event of a sudden stop. Remember that an untethered animal becomes a missile in the case of an accident.

The hardest part isn't always getting them there, it's convincing them it's time to go home.

Flying typically causes more anxiety and stress than car travel, so only fly pets if necessary. Speak to the airlines, as rules and regulations vary with the size and type of pet. Medications from a vet can manage motion sickness and anxiety. You should absolutely avoid travelling when it's hot. Confined conditions in cars can be a quick recipe for disaster.

Where are they going to stay?

Obviously check that the hotel, motel, caravan park or camping ground is animal friendly (look for a complete guide to pet-friendly accommodation). If you are able to involve your pet in your holiday as much as possible then it's potentially a win–win situation. They have a great time, while having your best mate there can only make the whole holiday more enjoyable and relaxing for you. Try not to leave pets alone in unfamiliar hotel rooms. It's stressful, lonely and definitely doesn't add up to a fun holiday. For that reason, outdoor (farm and beach) holidays are best suited to pets.

City holidays or visits to National Parks are not a good choice. Before you travel, the essentials should already be in place.

If they stay

Leaving your pets at home implies as much responsibility (if not more) as if they have gone away with you. You have a few options about how they are cared for while you're away.

They can be fed at home by a friend, neighbour or a professional feeding service. Unless a person is able to live in your house for the duration of the holiday, this is really only an option for cats. Dogs need more social interaction and exercise and if bored or lonely, they will look to escape. Regular feeding times and a dependable routine are essential if your pets are having the home-stay holiday. Not knowing who will come or when someone will come to feed and/or play with them causes unnecessary stress and increases the risk of the whole experience going sour.

Another option is to put your pet into a boarding kennel or cattery. This is the safest option as the animals are typically well supervised and do have some interaction with people and other pets. Before booking in, make a point of having a thorough tour to check out the quality of the housing, exercise areas and even the staff.

Your final option if your pet is staying behind is the farm stay, or pet holiday, option. Here, the pets go on their holiday and you go on yours. These services typically pick up the animals and drop them home after their holiday. This is fantastic for dogs that seem to thrive with the exercise and social life that this brings. It is an option best suited to dogs that are extraverted and active in the first place. Bear in mind that if your dog isn't this way inclined, and doesn't particularly like activity or socialising, then it could seem a little bit like boot-camp.

If they go

If your pet comes on holidays, then it will only work if you involve them as much as possible in the experience. Do your research before you get there and try and work in some pet-friendly activities to keep them entertained — this doesn't mean leaving the television on in the room. Chances are that pets (especially dogs) will be more active and spend more hours outdoors than usual. For that reason, issues like sunburn (on noses, ear tips and hairless bellies) and heat exhaustion should be considered. Dogs affected by arthritis will usually start to feel it in their joints after a few days of vigorous running and playing. Running in sand or sandy soils can also cause an irritation to your dog's feet if they aren't used to the surface. Sand gets between their toes and rubs like sandpaper. Constant licking of the

FIVE ★ HOLIDAY TIPS

★ You should always ensure there is plenty of water available for your pet. Dehydration is a big killer.

★★ You won't travel without a seat belt so make sure they travel safely too. A small crate, a harness or a barrier is essential.

★★★ Making regular travel stops will help the driver as well as the pet. They will be more relaxed if they have relieved themselves, stretched their legs and had a drink of water.

★★★★ Ensure your pet gets their normal food in boarding or on holidays. This prevents unpleasant gut upsets.

★★★★★ Have your pet checked by a vet before you go on holidays and know what diseases your pet might encounter. Prevent these where possible. Also ensure that you have your pet microchipped.

feet and red raw skin between the toes are common signs that their feet are irritated.

Most importantly, you need to identify any potential dangers that may be lurking in the area you are staying. The local vet will be a good, reliable source of information as to the things to look out for, as well as the best way to prevent them. Ticks, spiders, snakes and even water can pose a threat to your pet.

Paralysis ticks are a big risk for any pet that is holidaying along the east coast of Australia. The classic signs of paralysis: weak legs, difficulty breathing, vomiting and gagging, will take around 3-4 days to appear after the tick has attached itself. Ensure that you take some preventative measures against ticks if travelling to these areas.

Good flea control and worm prevention is an important courtesy to the other pet owners and, of course, their pets, as well as other people that may use the accommodation after you have left.

PLAYING IT SAFE

You want the relationship with your new pet to be many things. The number one priority should be that it's a safe and comfortable one, especially where kids are concerned.

A dog's behaviour towards children will almost always be different than their attitude towards adults. But why is that? Well, a child is the closest living creature in the house in terms of size, age and superiority. And as such, the person that they are least likely to be submissive to. But it is the job of the child and adults in the family to let the dog know at every opportunity that it is right at the bottom of the superiority ladder. This means training the dog to obey commands (sit, stay, drop, and so on), ensuring that it knows its place in the house (off furniture when told, not fed from the table, and so on) and always rewarding good behaviour with treats and praise. Dogs from a young age should be socialised with young children to enable them to get used to their size and, at times, unpredictable behaviour. Never forget that the best way to deal with aggressive behaviour is to prevent it in the first place.

But it's not just the dogs that need to have some training. Teaching kids how to behave around dogs is equally important. It reduces the risk of a dog experiencing fear and anxiety when confronted with a child. Kids should know to:

- be calm and gentle around dogs
- avoid teasing, poking, pulling or hitting dogs
- avoid dogs that growl or look scared
- avoid strange dogs where possible
- avoid dogs that have food or are eating
- avoid tug-o-war or other aggressive games with dogs
- never corner a dog
- don't run away from a dog if it approaches — stand still, turn sideways and let it sniff you

Kids under the age of five should be constantly supervised around pets. This is mostly to prevent unplanned and unintended contact that may result in tension. A child cornering a dog or playing with its food are classic examples. The ability to be able to monitor the development of the relationship is also important.

A baby will seem like an odd, alien-like object to a dog. After all, every other person that they have come in contact with walks on two legs and makes very controlled movements. But here is a four-legged gurgling creature that crawls, is unpredictable and at the same eye-height as your dog. Remember that it should be seen as a privilege by the dog for it to be in the baby's company. From the start, dogs should be rewarded for relaxed and appropriate behaviour. However, at the slightest indication of over-excitement or aggression, the dog should be told 'no' and sin-binned. Even though the baby is so small, its continual close contact with its parents make it seem an important and respected object to the dog.

Know the signs

Some dogs, often through no fault of their own, feel the need to be aggressive. Either they have been brought up that way or are so scared (and often cornered) that they think they need to defend themselves. Recognising the signs that a dog is feeling scared and may attack can prevent serious injuries. Look for the following signs:

- flattening of the ears
- lowering the tail
- raising the 'hackles' (the hair on the back of the neck and top of the shoulders)
- trembling
- urinating, defecating
- wide eyes

QUICK DOG TIP:
introducing yourself to a dog

They say first impressions are important. And this is how to make the best one with a dog. Firstly, kneel down and talk in a gentle, calm voice. Call him or her to you while holding out your hand flat and low with your palm facing up. Don't rush them, just let them come to you when they're ready. Let them sniff your hand and get comfortable with you before you pat them. Only ever stroke a new dog under the chin, on the neck or the tummy. Avoid patting an unfamiliar dog on the top of the head as to a scared dog (that might be from a bad home) it might look like you are trying to hit it.

TRAINING

Before you get out the stopwatch, clipboard and whistle and formulate a regime that aims to get your pet a berth in the 2012 Olympics, let's get it straight. We're talking about another sort of training. Training that teaches good behaviour and manners; and it can be super-important for you and your new pet.

The great thing is that it's easy to make it fun for both the pet and the owner. Training doesn't have to be, and shouldn't be, overcomplicated. What you should be aiming for is to establish a few basic commands that allow you to interact with your little mate and allow them to show off how intelligent they really are. This contact and communication does wonders for reinforcing the bond between the owner and their pet. The pet is made to feel like an important and valuable part of a relationship by obeying commands, fulfilling their part of the deal and then earning a reward. While the owner gains a responsive and interactive pet. Establishing a few handy phrases or actions means that despite what you might think, you can actually talk to your animals.

Training is one of those areas that makes us realise just how different animals are. But they are all the same in terms of when the training should take place — sooner rather than later. When your pet is able to respond to its name, it's ready to have training. Typically 12 weeks of age is the ideal time to start training dogs and cats.

Training dogs

Almost all dogs love food (very strongly in most cases), toys and games (such as chasing balls), and pats. When planning to train, work out what best motivates your dog. Typically food rewards combined with praise and pats will inspire most dogs to learn.

You should use food as the initial incentive. However, once your student has mastered the skill, it should only be used as an occasional treat. Not knowing when the treat will be earned becomes part of the game. This is appropriately called the poker machine principle, as it relies on your dog trying his luck over and over again until he hits the jackpot. It will also help to ensure that your dog doesn't balloon out in size as a result of his studies.

You don't have to get too carried away with training, but a knowledge of the basics is important. These will enable you to control and communicate with your dog for the rest of its life. Think of it as their primary school education. With these skills in the bag, then they've got the world at their little feet.

TIP

You've got to love the poker machine principle. Not giving a treat for good behaviour every time (making it a random event) keeps a lid on the waistline but maximises the fun.

What makes a good treat? Why not try dried liver pieces or special treat biscuits. The key is that the treat should be strong tasting and keep them coming back for more.

LESSON 1
The sit

In kindergarten, you learned all the basic stuff. Spelling, counting and being able to write your name. The basics set you up to do everything else after that. The same goes for the 'sit'. It's the building block for all other tricks.

1 Get your dogs attention by holding up a treat and calling his or her name.

2 With your dog standing in front of you, slowly move your hand with the treat up and over the top of their head.

3 Your dogs eyes will be fixed on the treat and follow it right back. He or she will naturally sit so they can watch it move over their head.

4 The moment they sit, give them plenty of praise ... oh, and the treat.

Do this over and over again and they will realise that it's the sitting action that gets the reward. The great thing about the 'sit' command is that it's an attention grabber. If your dog is barking or misbehaving then you can use 'sit' as a way of getting them to stop and listen to you. They will always respond to the command as they know there is a fair chance of some food at the end of it.

LESSON 2
The drop

1 First get your dog into the sitting position (see lesson 1).

2 With a new treat in your hand, slowly slide it along the ground between your dog's two front legs and towards their belly.

3 In order to follow the treat, your dog will have to lower their nose and eye level. Without even thinking about it, they will lie down.

4 As soon as they are lying comfortably on the ground, give them the reward. Repeat this a few times until they get it.

Avoid training straight after a meal. They are usually sleepy and looking forward to a rest at this time. The best time for class is between meals. They will be more responsive and desperate for that reward if they are at least a little hungry.

LESSON 3
The stay

1 Get your dog into the sitting or lying down position (see lesson 1 or 2).

2 With your dog's attention on you, put your hand up in the 'stop' position (palm flat and fingers pointing up), say the word 'stay' and take a step back. Return immediately and give your pet a reward.

3 Do step 2 again but this time take a few extra steps. The aim here is to increase the distance between the two of you and the time that your dog must wait.

4 Remember to reward them when they stay the distance!

Socialisation — being around as many other dogs and people of all ages and sizes — is as important as training. So these training steps are best performed in conjunction with playing and mixing with other two- and four-legged creatures. So put a politician to shame by getting out there and 'meeting and greeting' everyone.

LESSON 4
The 'okay'

The 'okay' command is a really handy one. It enables you to tell your dog that it's okay to do something but most importantly encourages a dog to seek approval before it takes a treat or its meal.

1 Start by getting your dog into the sit position (see lesson 1) then say 'stay' as you edge your way back a few steps. Your dog should be waiting patiently.

2 This time though, instead of returning to give the treat, place it on the ground. Say 'stay', put your hand up in the 'stop' position and edge a few steps away from the treat. Say 'stay' occasionally to reinforce the idea.

3 When your dog has waited for at least 10 seconds, say 'okay' in a happy, excited tone and drop your hands by your sides. Your dog should race forward and grab the treat.

4 The real key to this command is the tone that you say the word 'okay' in. Said in a firm, serious tone it will sound too much like 'stay'. So make it upbeat, fun and happy — after all, it's the green light to eat that your dog has been waiting for.

Don't feel as though you have to use the words 'sit', 'drop', 'stay', and so on. Provided you always use the same cue you can make the key word whatever you like. And kids, this is not a licence to get your pets responding to swear words.

LESSON 5
The shake hands
(a.k.a. The high-5)

This is a bit of a show-off trick. Even though this trick has no real behavioural benefit, it's something that will impress your mates. And I seriously reckon this is one of the favourite tricks for a dog — it's low-effort, easy and almost always gets the reward. It also presents a great opportunity for you to vary the key word. You can substitute 'shake hands' for anything that will get a laugh when your dog raises his paw. After all, your dog could be giving you a 'high-5', a punch, or even pointing at who he or she thinks is good looking, hot or 'the boss'.

1 Start by getting your dog in the 'sit' position (see lesson 1).

2 Hold the treat in one hand and using your free hand, gently reach down and put your hand behind your dog's paw.

3 As you give the paw a gentle tap towards you, say your key word and give the treat.

4 Gradually decrease the amount that you need to touch the paw and work on just reaching out with your hand in that direction. You should get to the stage where you just need to say your key word and the dog will respond.

Have fun with this one, but remember, if your dog is going to produce the response on command, you must be consistent with the key word. So, for example, use either 'shake hands', 'high-5', or 'who's hot?'. But only use one and stick with it.

Training for cats

Many people that have owned cats and grown to know their personalities, would think that the words 'cat' and 'training' should not be seen in the same sentence. What I see and hear day after day from my clients, is that we don't so much as train them, as they show us how we could be better managing them. It's very much on their own terms. But that's cats and that's part of their charm. You almost can't help but find their mystery, confidence and arrogance intriguing.

However, knowing how best to manipulate their behaviour to be the most appropriate for our needs is the key. Like a business deal, you may have to meet the cat halfway in order to get a satisfactory result. So let's look at what you can do.

Scratching

Scratching is a natural behaviour that is used by cats to not only keep their claws in good condition, but also to rub their scent (from their pads) on objects they see as being worthy of their cat cologne. Because it's an instinctive behaviour, you're probably not going to be able to eliminate it completely. By the same token though, your pristine leather couch wasn't around thousands of years ago when Puss' great-grandfather learned how to scratch. So it looks like time to compromise.

First of all, you should learn how to trim your cat's nails using a proper pair of nail clippers. Having them cut short to the point just below the 'quick' (blood vessels and nerves) means that their weapons of mass destruction are downsized — making the shredding of your furniture a less successful activity. This will buy you some time while you work on the long-term plan.

Ideally, you want to transfer this scratching behaviour from the centre of your living room to a scratching post. This post acts as a bit of a sacrifice to the feline god of scratching. You let your cat tear this apart while the rest of your furniture is left unscathed. In a perfect world, cats should find the post's surface highly appealing and then leave your furniture alone. Mostly though, they need to be pointed in the right direction. The best way to do this is to place your scratching post next to the piece of furniture that the cat finds most appealing. Your cat should be drawn to the post. If they become distracted though, and drift back to the original scratching site, then give a firm 'no' and put them back on the post. When you see your cat using the scratching post, give them a gentle pat and praise them. As they become comfortable with the scratching post, slowly move it further away from the furniture. Over the next few days and weeks, increase the distance until the scratching post now sits in a convenient spot for both you and the cat. Cats that spend a lot of time outdoors may find a tree more satisfying, so that may also be a workable compromise if the outdoor area is safe.

TIP

The basic rule of cats and litter trays is number of cats + 1 = number of litter trays. Be sure to space them around — cats like their privacy too.

Cats are naturally playful animals. So give them an outlet like a scratching post or climbing pole and they'll love you forever.

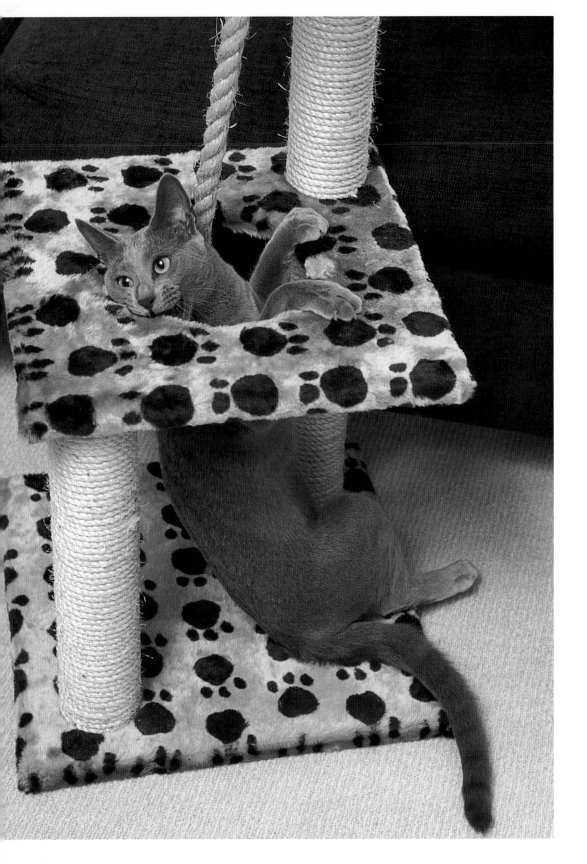

Cruising for a bruising. Territorial disputes are an all-too common event in urban areas.

Territorial disputes

It's 2 am, you lie comfortably under your warm blankets, relaxed and dreamy. It's quiet too, but suddenly something has woken you, and the suburb's dog population, who roar in excitement and expectation ... then ... the noise again ... that piercing duet that sounds like two stretched violin strings being scraped with a cheese-grater. For the classical urban dispute is on again between two stubborn felines intent on not taking a backward step from the piece of Doris Smith's back garden that they both consider their own. Some cats seem unable to stay out of trouble, seemingly always nursing war wounds from a late night scuffle over territory. Day after

day, their owners bring the battered and bruised to me, each with a different story of a battle fought away from prying eyes, for a piece of land already owned by a two-legged creature but much in dispute by those with four legs. Like a mosquito drawn to a bug-zapper at night, so too are felines drawn to fight. But why? What does it mean to you? And what can be done about it? For starters, you can make your cat less likely to enter the ring by keeping it inside as much as possible. You should certainly keep the cat inside at night, which is when most fights occur.

Cats are not unique in wanting to guard their piece of turf. Much like a person aims to own their own house and feel secure and fulfilled in it, a cat will instinctively look to mark out their own territory. Having a clearly defined piece of land is something that all cats look to achieve. It doesn't have to be a massive estate, most city-slicker cats are happy to have just a small courtyard or even a room. However, they all share one feature — it must be theirs and theirs alone. There are four signals used to mark territory. A cat may either spray urine, leave faeces, put scratch marks on trees and fence posts, or rub the scent from skin glands in his cheeks onto territorial objects. Even though these marks are instinctive, some of them are definitely not pleasant, especially if they appear in your house. Urine spraying is the most common form of marking and can become a real headache for cat owners, especially when that rich odour of cat urine fills the air in the lounge room. If this starts to occur in your house, then you need to work though this checklist:

- Is your cat desexed? Entire (not desexed) cats (especially males) are more likely to spray as they feel a need to mark out a large territory for mating. Desexing takes away the sex hormones that cause this behaviour and makes a cat more calm and less concerned with enforcing their presence.

- Is another cat trespassing? If a neighbour's cat comes into your cat's yard or house and sprays, then your cat will immediately do the same. Keep other cats away by having a water-spray bottle (or a hose) on hand to drench it. You can also try to create a 'force-field' around your house and yard by using a smell to act as a deterrent to any cat wanting to make a land-claim on your backyard. Mothballs placed a few feet apart in a ring around the yard can sometimes help the problem. They contain a strong smelling component that is repulsive to your average cat. A commercially available cat deterrent spray may also be another option worth exploring.

- Are your cats house-trained? Do you have enough litter trays? Obviously, if a cat doesn't know where to go, or is uncomfortable about going in the 'right place' then accidents will often result. Make sure you have one more litter tray than you have cats. This will ensure that there is a private and clean place for each and every cat to use. You should also try a few different places around the house and see what works. Try a few different types of litter and see which one your cat seems most happy with. The way to tell is to notice how quickly and comfortably your cat goes when they approach the litter tray.

- Is there a human trespasser? Cats are incredibly sensitive and emotional creatures and any change in the mini-society of their home can upset them greatly. Having a new baby in the family, or a friend coming to stay, can cause a great deal of anxiety in the cat and make it want to mark out its territory.

If you have eliminated all of the above as a cause of spraying, then the most likely reason is anxiety. Cats that feel insecure and unsure in their surroundings will look to make themselves feel more at home. Unfortunately, the main way they do this is by making the house smell like them. Anxiety is a very treatable condition in cats. Pheromone sprays and 'plug-ins' are available which release a specific feline smell that pacifies cats. In severe cases, medication will certainly make a difference, but this should be on the recommendation of your local vet or animal behaviour specialist.

Digging

Some cats become keen excavators in their spare time. This is often the result of boredom or in response to the urge to go to the toilet. Either way, it can cause damage to the garden and flowerpots. The interesting fact is, though, that cats are quite poor diggers as their claws are more suited to hunting than digging. Simply covering the surface with small stones will be enough to deter the average cat from its earth-moving. Also, ensure that there are clean litter trays available and the type of litter used is liked by the cat.

No-go areas

Cats are not easily confined to a designated area. After all, they combine an inquisitive mind with 'go-anywhere' agility. From a young age you need to be firm with the areas that your cat can and cannot access. There are some that are dangerous (such as hot stoves) while some areas are places where cats are unwelcome (such as beds, pillows and furniture). When you see your kitten in these

What do you do when your favourite outdoor table becomes the preferred perching position for puss? Make it a no-go area.

'no-go' areas you must be quick to react. The best thing to do is carry a set of keys in your pocket and simply toss them on the floor near where your cat is, and shouldn't be. The surprise of the noise should cause the cat to make a hasty exit. Do this often enough and your cat will surely get the message. A water-spray bottle could also be used. Remember, the key with this exercise is to only startle your cat — safety is the first priority.

Toilet training

With all the showerings of affection, toys and treats, you could excuse a young pet for wanting to give a little in return. And they say the key to gift giving is timing and picking out just the right thing. Which is probably why any small mistakes in toilet training seem to happen on the most prominent, whitest, or most valuable floor covering, and just as you are expecting visitors.

This behaviour obviously has implications for us as pet owners. However, it can also affect pets' lives as well. Take for example, a kitten that came into my family when I was thirteen years old. This tortoiseshell kitten was a petite, timid little thing, and being surrounded by three brawling brothers and an 'amorous' black poodle probably didn't help change this in a hurry. I should point out that she had been an unplanned arrival, dropped off at Dad's work to be 'put to sleep' because the owner's kids had decided that they 'just didn't like it'. As is often the case for unexpected arrivals, a name was not forthcoming for the new cat. This was a significant piece of bad luck for this torty kitten as it was about to find out. You see, this cat being still quite young and being switched between homes was yet to truly master the art of 'toilet training'. Or at least that was the excuse. For with regular monotony, and with a sense of timing not unlike that seen in a Rolex watch, kitty could and would unload. And not just anywhere. The chosen 'drop-off' time and place was determined by when and where dinner guests were to be seated and at what stage of dinner they were at. Typically, kitty would release three days of pent-up frustration under the dining table, on top of Mum's intricate floor rug. The sheer beauty of her simple act was that it was always placed within inches of the stiletto-clad flicking feet of the most precious dinner guest at the time the main course was delivered to the table. How she got in under the table, had the sheer mental fortitude and composure to unload, and then escape before the aromas from beneath the table unceremoniously mixed with those coming from above was truly worthy of accolades. Indeed, she was never caught in the act. Instead, she received an award of another sort — the gift of a name. She was named 'Poo-Cat'. Quite an honour when your surname is Brown.

Toilet training need not be such an ordeal. It's simply a matter of predicting when they will want to go and do their business. And no, I'm not expecting you to get out the tea leaves, crystal balls and astrology charts. You just need to know that young pets are most likely to want to go after waking, playing or eating. So at these times, and at the last moment before you put them to bed, escort your pet to their designated 'drop-zone'. For cats this would be the litter tray (or a safe outdoor area). Once there, place your cat in the litter and leave it to be alone until the little 'package' has been delivered. Your cat may need a little redirecting and encouragement if it strays away from the litter tray, but persevere as they will eventually get the idea. What you should never do however, is place his or her food and water near the litter tray. Cats are incredibly precious creatures and won't ever

want to urinate or defecate near their dinner; which makes perfect sense to me.

If you have one cat, you should have two litter trays. This is handy, at least when your cat is learning, as it ensures they always have a litter tray close by; and if it's fussy about where to go, there should be something to its liking. Where this is crucial is when you have more than one cat. Most cats refuse to use the same tray as a different feline (they are precious after all), so having a choice of another with clean litter, and a back-up, is crucial if you want to avoid accidents along the way.

The same general principle applies for dogs. Instead of a litter tray (although this can be done if you live in an apartment), try a secluded part of the garden where the sight and smell won't be a concern. When your dog performs and does his or her business, then praise your dog.

The key with both of these situations is to simply reinforce where the 'right' place is to go. It will take time and patience and there will be the occasional lapse in concentration, even resulting in a Poo-Cat experience of your own. But just go with it and know that you will get there in the end, even if it takes months rather than days.

POO-CAT FOOTNOTE
There was an interesting experience at a dinner party a few months after Poo-Cat earned her name. For just as dinner was being served, Mum bumped a fork on to the floor. With everyone's attention drawn below the table, it was all too easy to observe a black and white flash making a quick escape. When the feline had left the room, a 'calling card' remained on the rug. And outside the tortoiseshell Poo-Cat peered in through the glass, alone but for her unfortunate and undeserved name.

CAT TRAINING:
Teaching your cat to use the toilet

In the same way as you are right now — I thought this sounded ridiculous when I first heard it. The thought of puss boldly positioning herself on the porcelain to do her business is too ridiculous to contemplate, let alone teaching your own cat to do it. And that's exactly why I'm going to explain how to do it. There are advantages of course; not having to empty the litter tray and knowing that at least she will not leave the seat up (that fur left on the toilet seat may require some explanation though). Each step should be taken slowly and only advance to the next level when you are sure that they are ready (at least a week for each stage is usually required). First, train your cat to use a litter tray positioned on the bathroom floor. Use the standard toilet training technique already outlined. Once he or she is comfortable with the litter tray, move the litter tray so it now sits on top of the toilet seat which has the cover over it. Ensure they are then comfortable with it there. This step is crucial, as it gets your cat used to jumping up onto the toilet. Now, using a smaller litter tray or bowl, place it inside the toilet bowl. Your cat will see it just beneath the seat and should be able to sit on the seat and go from there. Once he or she seems entirely comfortable with that, remove the litter altogether, so that puss is peeing freely into the bowl. Finally, teach them to flush! I would recommend disinfecting the toilet before you claim it back.

HOW TO MAKE YOUR CAT LOVE YOUR DOG

The ongoing power struggle between canine and feline has turned many backyards into battlefields over the years. So, after all this time, is it possible to achieve peace and turn loathers into lovers? Here's 10 easy ice-breaking suggestions to help your cat see a different side to your dog. But remember, just as it is the case in human relationships, every dog and cat situation is different. So be prepared that not every piece of counselling advice will work. Time will often be the best healer of all.

How to ease any initial tension

Don't dine together As romantic as it seems to enjoy dinner together, it's an aperitif to an argument. So separate eating areas will help. Food is seen as a sacred object to both cats and dogs and competition for it is all too common. Letting your cat 'enjoy' their dinner rather than defend the bowl from pilfering pooches means much less tension for the next 24 hours.

Play favourites Much of the angst between a dog and cat arises from competition, and the competition for your affection is high on the list of priorities. But if you can make them feel like the war is already won, then the chances of peace increase. Spending quality time alone with each pet is the key. Make them feel like the favourite and they won't be nearly as concerned about the other 'hanger-on'.

Have 'safe-zones', which are dog-only and cat-only areas Having your dog able to rummage through your cat's bed and food bowls isn't a foundation for a loving bond. Having a place that your cat can run to that is a dog 'no-go' area is essential. A 'safe-zone' helps your cat feel more relaxed and comfortable in their normal surroundings knowing that there is a place to go if the need arises.

Allow the cat to watch from the sidelines Playtime for your dog is the highlight of the day and the highpoint in terms of exuberance and excitement. Don't throw balls or toys anywhere near where your cat might be resting or retreating. Your cat can all too easily become part of your dog's game which will far from impress puss.

Starting afresh

Start them young If a kitten can have positive and relaxed experiences with a dog then chances are that the comfortable feelings towards a dog will last a lifetime. The same goes for young puppies with older cats. The socialisation period (6–12 weeks for a kitten and 8–16 weeks for a pup) is when a pet forms its own opinions on its surroundings. This is when the crucial and gentle first introductions should be made. Typically, if the right kind of introduction is made during this time, the likelihood of ongoing tension is minimal.
First impressions Carefully managing that crucial first meeting is essential. This applies to any age of cat or dog. Just don't rush it. The new cat or dog should first be allowed to acclimatise to the new surroundings without any threat or intrusion. Separate them to a different part of the house, so they may be heard and smelt by the existing pet, but not seen. When both cat and

dog seem comfortable, then an initial meeting at a safe distance may be attempted. Dogs don't seem to know the meaning of 'gentle' when meeting a cat, so place the dog on a short leash and keep it under control. While holding both animals, the interactions should be relaxed and you should reward calm behaviour with treats. Over a number of encounters, increase the time spent and the proximity to each other. Remember that you must separate them at the first sign of fear. This is an especially important time for a kitten. Cats must have positive experiences in early life if they are to willingly interact with a dog later on.

If the feud has been long running

Build some trust Make no mistake, this is difficult and will take some time. The key is to have controlled interactions at a safe and comfortable distance. The dog should be made to sit (while attached to a short leash) a few feet away from the cat. The cat should be held and stroked while they build a level of comfort with the dog's presence. Doing this while watching television is often a good start. If the cat struggles and frets then move further away from the dog. Over time, lessen the hold on the cat and also the distance between the combatants.

Sealing the deal

Associate the D.O.G. with G.O.O.D. When there is at the very least a mutual respect for each other, this is the way to take the relationship to the next level. With the cat as close to the dog as possible, lavish the cat with pats while the dog receives the occasional treat for calm, relaxed behaviour. Extend the sessions for up to 10 minutes. Have 30 seconds break and then start another session. Over time you should aim to move them closer and closer together. The beauty of this technique is that it teaches your cat a pleasant association response. Your cat will begin to see your dog as the site, and possible source, of affection and your dog will know that calm behaviour around the cat results in rewards.

To really turn on the charm

Make the dog wear the cat's favourite cologne Rubbing some catnip plant or extract (also available in a spray) onto the dog's collar might just make the dog seem more interesting or even alluring to a flirtatious feline!

finding a suitable pet

Finding a suitable pet to match your needs can be one of the most unique processes that you will ever go through. What may seem like a simple matter of tracking down a friendly-enough ball of fluff can require all the planning, strategy, insight and knowledge of a military operation. Luckily, the whole experience should be a whole lot of fun if done the right way. That perfect pet could be anything and it could be lurking anywhere, and it takes a special kind of person to put together the pieces and track down your new special 'little' person.

There are three integral parts to the puzzle: what you require as an owner; what you should be looking for in a breeder, pet store or pound; and what you should be looking for in a pet.

If you don't know your ragdolls from your ridgebacks, then it's going to make it difficult to make an informed choice and prevent dishonest retailers from pulling the wool, fur or feathers, over your eyes. Use this book as a guide — it contains all the essential information you require. Your vet should also be able to give you useful tips on what to look out for in your particular area.

Work out what suits you

If you're looking for a pet for a child, a pet tortoise may seem like a good idea. However, when you consider that a tortoise can live up to 60 years, the thought of your child reaching retirement at the same time as his pet does may not be the best option. Long-lived pets for kids often become pets for parents, while some pets are simply not suitable for children. There are many examples of pets that don't quite fit your situation. When choosing your pet, consider the amount of space available, the time that you will be able to spend with your pet, the level of attention required, the cost involved, whether the pet will be around children, and your stage of life. The pet should fit the bill on all of these considerations.

Lets face it, even a shark's babies are cute. But they do grow up, and some pets can develop into quite a handful. So before you get bombarded with a thousand choices, know what you're after and try to stay with these general choices.

The only person to ever legitimately own two of every pet was Noah. And unless you have the inside word on a poor long-range weather forecast and a large boat, then you're probably not justified to collect every pet you lay your eyes on. Remember that it's a long-term commitment, both emotionally and financially. If you're not completely sure if the pet is right for you, then you're better off leaving it. Whatever it takes, try not to get emotionally attached to a pet when you first meet it — keep a steely determination and limit your eye contact if necessary. Look over it, talk to the owner about it and then put it back. Do not give it a name — it's a thousand times harder to say goodbye to something with a name.

Hermit crabs make a terrific choice for those people who like their pets with a little bit of artistic flair and colour.

When looking over an animal, the pressure can be enormous. Everyone will be throwing in their opinion, there will be other people looking at the pets (that might also want your choice), and the breeders or store owners will be telling you that they are just 'walking out the door'. Among this, it's easy to lose your cool and be forced into a rushed decision. So, walk yourself out the door instead. If you are close to making your choice, take a break. Find somewhere quiet and talk it over with family and friends. What you should do will become clear once you have a quiet moment to work it all out.

Buying a pet is obviously not something you rush into. When you do decide to bring home a pet for the first time, make sure everything is prepared for the new arrival. Have a designated sleeping area (which isn't your bed) and a place for feeding. Changing things about and seeming disorganised will only make the first few important nights more stressful than the fun times that they should be.

MEET THE PARENTS

It can be a bit like meeting the in-laws of your new boyfriend or girlfriend. To find the pet is one thing, to survive meeting the breeders or the pet store that it's from can be another experience entirely. At the most basic level you have three options as to where you find your pet: a pet store, a breeder, or a pound. Each have their advantages and disadvantages.

Survival guide to the breeder

Breeders are like New Year's Eve parties and birthdays — you have good and bad ones, and (sometimes) you just can't avoid them. As a general rule though, breeders breed animals because they love them. Because they become such a massive part of their life, they always strive for the best for their beloved 'sons' and 'daughters'. Quality breeders will always take special care to ensure that the animals they sell are healthy and not prone to long-term problems. But remember, they won't give up their 'children' to just anyone. You will often have to prove your credentials and genuine love of their animals before they allow you to take a pet home. Don't be surprised if you're asked to dinner or subjected to a rigorous interview before you are deemed fit to adopt. Try not to see this as an inconvenience, but rather as a way to meet the 'parents'. After all, it's a sign that you are taking home something special. If you are simply looking for a pet and have no plans for showing

So hard to resist. Despite every part of you wanting to take it home — ask yourself 'is it really for you?'.

Having a potential pet's relative close to hand can give you an insight on how your pet might look and, importantly, behave.

or breeding, then make sure you tell them this. There may be no point in spending thousands of dollars on a potential show grand champion, when the only 'show' it will see will be on your television. A breeder is able to give you full details on the puppy or kitten, its parents and the all important details to do with its eyesight, hearing, hip scores, elbows and pedigree. You may pay more for this detail, but it can help to provide some peace of mind not available from pet stores and pounds. Chances are that there will be an immediate relative on hand (mother or father, or

even a sibling from a previous litter). These animals are invaluable to use as a guide as to how the pet might look and especially, behave, when fully grown. You know exactly what you're getting when you buy it from the factory outlet.

The downside

Don't fall into the trap of believing that pedigree and breeding are everything. Thankfully, that way of thinking ended long ago, and genetics has shown that a bit of variety in the gene pool does a lot of good for dogs and cats too.

Breeders spend their life around animals and understandably accumulate a lot of knowledge about the pets they breed. However, all feeding guides, health tips and exercise regimes that are recommended by breeders should be cleared with your vet first. That way, your vet can ensure that your pet is getting all the nutrients and care it needs and it will avoid the development of any nutritional deficiencies, growth problems or health issues.

Most breeders certainly want you to have a member of their close-knit family. However, they will make you work for it. Typically breeders live on the outskirts of the major cities, and will take extra time to get to know you and how much you will care for their pet. Just remember though, that it will be worth it in the long term despite the short-term inconvenience.

The brief

A breeder will usually be able to provide you with a healthy, well socialised and well-cared for pet. They will however, make you pay (and work) for the extra care and could even limit your future plans for the animal. Always check any nutritional and exercise advice by a breeder with your vet.

Encouraging your kitten to play from a young age makes for a happier and healthier cat in later years. Have a selection of toys on hand to keep them amused for hours.

Survival guide to the pet store

Despite debate over whether it's right to 'shop' for a companion, pet shops are a popular place to purchase a pet. They offer a wide selection of animals and are often conveniently located. If you do decide that a pet store is the way to go, the pet should already have had their first vet health check and vaccination by the time they are purchased. Puppies and kittens should be at least 8 weeks old with no visible signs of disease or sickness.

Ask as many questions as possible to the store employees. Use their answers to gauge how competent and knowledgeable the store is. If they seem unsure about details relating to the animal's age, history, health and that of its parents, then typically these are the stores that sell pets more for profit than for the love of it. Try to find a pet store that is passionate about its work, its animals and always puts their health and welfare above profits.

The downside

Reputable pet shops exist, so it's vital you take your time finding one, if this is the way you're leaning.

The first few months of a dog's or cat's life is best spent with as many other dogs and cats, with socialising being the number one objective. This just isn't possible inside a glass container. Bringing a bunch of young animals together in one place, all from different litters and homes, makes it convenient for someone looking for a pet. However, it also makes it extremely easy for any viruses or bugs that are around to do the same. It's why a thorough vet check is important before you take your pet home.

You will almost certainly have no way of seeing the parents or other relatives of the animal you are contemplating buying. Watching the behaviour of immediate, fully-grown relatives is an invaluable way of looking into the future to see how your pet will behave (and look) when fully grown.

The brief

The key is to shop around. There are undoubtably more risks associated with pet stores than breeders, so always insist on a thorough vet check. Place a lot of emphasis on the quality of the pet store when making your final choice.

Survival guide to the pound

Quite simply, if you are not moved by what you see at the pound, you should be classified as an immoveable object. You will be confronted with potentially hundreds of animals, all in desperate need of a home. Whereas before, you may have *wanted* to take a pet home from a breeder or pet store, you will probably feel like you *need* to provide a home to an animal from the pound. But as before, the 'Noah' rule applies.

Be aware that a pet from a pound is certainly not suitable for everyone, and not every pound pet will be suitable for you. If you are lucky enough to meet your match, it is potentially a big win–win situation. The pet needs a home and your home needs a pet. If it works, it will certainly be one of the more rewarding experiences. They make relatively cheap pets, as most are usually fully grown and will certainly already be desexed, microchipped, vaccinated and checked over by a vet. And by choosing an older dog, you avoid the costs and time-consuming aspects of puppyhood. If you are a busy person, this may be a big positive, as the ordeals of house-training, teething and desexing are avoided with more mature pets.

The downside

Looking at the pound issue on the surface, it would seem like a great way to find a pet. And I do wish there was no downside, however, at least once a week I see the consequences of a pound pet that just doesn't fit in. There really is a significant risk in obtaining an animal from a shelter, unless you are able to say for sure how and why it got there. Some animals may certainly be abandoned or be victims of circumstance when the owners couldn't pay for their medical treatment, or in more depressing cases, of abuse or starvation, and these can make suitable and manageable pets. However, a significant number have run away from home or behaved in such a way that their owners have had to surrender them. It is these animals that may prove difficult to re-home successfully. Behavioural problems such as anxiety, escapism (digging, jumping), or even aggression can sometimes be remedied. However, many are not dramatically altered without medication or long-drawn out behavioural treatment. Put simply, providing a new home to one of these pets will most likely only end up prolonging their confusion with the world. I would love to be able to tell you that all pound pets are wonderful. However, it's not fair on a family (with young children) full of expectations for their new pet to have to endure countless problems that make living with the animal an impossibility.

There are many unknowns with pound pets. It's often difficult to truly determine a pet's age when it is brought into the pound with little history. There may be fears and phobias or even food fetishes or preferences that you won't know about until you get it home. At the very least, insist on taking the pet away from all the other animals, so that you may more accurately determine the animal's true personality.

The brief

Finding a suitable pound pet is certainly possible. It just requires some consideration of your needs and their personality. Most importantly, don't rush in. Watch the pet you're after intently and rely on the advice of the staff to assess the true personality of that animal. If you get it right, it's a truly rewarding experience for you and your new mate.

Tips to help you through

There are no guarantees in life, especially when you are dealing with little lives. However, there are some ways to minimise the risk so that you can go close to truly knowing what you're getting. Like a good detective does, gaining as much information as possible will help see you through.

A number of breeders and pet stores will offer you a 24-hour period in which you are able to take the pet home and then have it checked out by your vet. If there is something amiss or unsuitable discovered, then you usually have the option of returning the pet for a refund. I have seen some situations where a heart defect, a hip problem or even a case of cat flu has gone undetected until the animal has been taken to a vet. Obviously with the extra contact, the emotional bond increases and it may be hard to return the pet if the problem is serious. However, in that event, at least knowing the problem from the start will help.

At some stage during the pet-purchasing process, I am sure you will feel like you are being examined as to your suitability as a parent (especially when dealing with breeders). However, you should be the one examining them. Don't be shy to ask questions and inspect how cleanly and professionally they run their operation. Clean surroundings decrease the risk of animals getting sick. An establishment that cares about the little things, is more likely to value the growth, development and wellbeing of the animals.

A young dog, cat, rabbit and ferret must be vaccinated in order to avoid disease. Puppies and kittens must be given their crucial first shot between 6–8 weeks. Worming in these pets should be carried out every three weeks until six months of age. Insist on being shown proof that this has actually been carried out.

Finally, asking plenty of questions not only gives you information about the pet, but also information on how much the breeder or pet store knows (and indeed cares) about their animals. Following are a selection of questions that you should ask.

How old is the animal?

Younger animals might look cuter, but they are heavily reliant on care and attention. Most importantly though, they need to be with their mother for long enough to gain sufficient immunity from her to be resistant to all sorts of nasty bugs. Never buy an animal that is less than 6 weeks old. It's likely to not have been weaned from its mother properly, and will be weak and prone to infections. Wait until they are between 6–8 weeks old. By the same token, an animal bought when it's older than 12 weeks of age is at risk of being anti-social if it has been kept by itself, or with just a few other animals and hasn't been able to experience the 'real world'.

What is known about the parents?

Because a large proportion of pet health problems are passed on from generation to generation, knowing the health of the parents can go close to predicting how the youngster will go when he or she matures. Much like people, how the parents behave will often give an indication (but not a guarantee) as to what to expect from the offspring.

Be a pet detective — don't be too shy to ask questions about your prospective purchase.

What testing has been undertaken?

At the most basic level, a full vet check is vital. When there are valuable animals involved, or the breeders wish to be thorough, a more complete evaluation is possible and should be encouraged. Hips and elbows may be 'scored' to check for any evidence of structural problems. Eyes may be checked for vision and any evidence of genetic eye diseases like PRA (progressive retinal atrophy, an eye disease that causes premature blindness). Hearing can be evaluated, especially in those dogs prone to deafness such as dalmatians and bull terriers. Ultrasound can even be used to ensure there aren't any pre-existing kidney or liver problems, although this is usually reserved for those breeds prone to these abnormalities. All testing should be encouraged, as it is a sign that the breeders are looking to eliminate diseases from the bloodlines of their animals.

How has the animal been behaving?

Is it quiet or loud? An attention seeker or does it keep to itself? Even though the animal is most likely quite young when you first encounter it, many behaviour patterns and personality traits are already clear.

Has the animal had any health problems?

It's often hard to get an honest answer to this question, but you never know your luck. At the very least, asking the question shows you care.

THE PE(S)T INSPECTION

As they say, it's not just looks that count. You will amaze yourself, and those around you, by how much you can tell about an animal with just a few simple checks that until now were only known to the experts — your friends will be quizzing you on why you've been keeping that vet degree quiet for so many years. If you think you've found the pet you're after, don't even think about taking it home without your own, quick on-site pet inspection. It's obviously not as complex and thorough as the check your vet can and should provide, but it can rule in or rule out animals before you make any emotional (or financial) bond. And you are so much better off deciding early on than finding out a problem later.

The general check

The best technique is to start at the nose and work your way back from there.

Nose

The nose should not be running. Any green mucus present is a sign of disease. Watery discharges may be a sign of an early viral infection or allergies. The nose should usually be cold and wet. A dry nose is okay, provided there are no other signs of sickness.

Mouth

The animal's breath should smell clean and not offensive. For dogs, the classic puppy-breath smell should last until about 2–3 months of age — enjoy it while it lasts as the years of dog breath or tuna breath in cats are all ahead of you. The teeth should be free of any discolouration (especially if the animal is young). The appearance of the teeth will depend on the age and type of animal. The gums should be pink, except in those animals with pigmented gums. The gum-line that is in contact with teeth should not be red and sore. If there is a red line on the gums at their point of contact with the teeth, then a bacterial or viral infection is possible. Make a quick check on the roof of the mouth to be sure there isn't a cleft palate (a split in the hard palate).

Teeth

Some of us never want to own up to how old we truly are. However, it can be crucial when you are buying a pet. Obviously the best way to work out an animal's age is to ask its owner. Those people selling dogs and cats should not remove a puppy or kitten from its mother until at least 6 weeks of age. Any earlier and they risk not gaining all the possible immunity from their mother. If there is some uncertainty then these handy tips might

help. Remember, like us, dogs and cats have two sets of teeth during a lifetime. The first set (the 'temporary' or 'baby' teeth) are recognised by being small, narrow and, looking at your furniture and hands, sharp as well.

These should all be present with no gaps by 6 weeks of age. From about 8 weeks of age, the fun of teething begins. Their urges are to chew anything and everything as a way to stimulate the 'permanent' or 'adult' teeth to come through. These begin to come through first with the front (incisor) teeth, then the large back molar teeth and finally with the large fang-like canine teeth. The front incisors should start to be seen at 12 weeks of age, the back molar teeth emerge at 16 weeks, while the fang teeth start to come through at 20 weeks. All teeth are through by 6 months of age. To determine the age of a dog or cat that is older than 6 months, you rely more on their body size and the wear on the teeth. Normal eating will wear the teeth down slowly. If an animal is an obsessive bone chewer or stick chaser, then their teeth will say that they are older than they really are.

A mighty bite

Checking the bite, or how well the upper and lower jaws come together, can be a handy test. Animals that have teeth that 'miss' each other, inevitably have problems chewing their food properly and keeping their teeth clean as there is no brushing effect from the chewing action. In pets whose teeth grow continuously (like rabbits and guinea pigs), it is an absolute must for the teeth to line up. If they don't, then there is no way for the top and bottom teeth to wear each other down. Their fangs will keep on growing to an unmanageable length, making eating, and even

grooming, impossible. With the mouth closed, lift up the lips and inspect where the upper and lower jaw sit. The row of upper teeth should sit directly on top of the row of lower teeth. When they open their mouth, watch to see that the jaws open freely and then come to rest on top of one another once again.

Eyes

They say that the eyes are the window on the soul — so make sure those windows are clear, bright and shiny. The eyes, and particularly the pupils, should appear identical in size and shape, with the pupils in the middle of the eye. They should open freely and not be held partially closed. The whites of the eyes should be just that — not bloodshot or discoloured. There should be no watering of the eyes or pussy discharge. Large clumps of sleep in the inner corner of the eyes, or tears down the face, may be an indication of blocked tear ducts, which may or may not be fixable. Under no circumstances should eyelashes touch the eye, these will cause a dramatic and serious irritation.

Ears

As handy as it might be as an excuse for disobedience, wax in your pet's ears is simply not normal. Especially when there are large amounts and it's a nasty dark colour. The inside of the ears should be clean and relatively free of wax and odour. A strong, pungent odour indicates a bacterial or fungal infection which, if occurring at a young age, makes long term problems likely. A large amount of dark wax with some pinhead-sized white spots moving among the wax most likely indicates an infestation with ear mites. These are surprisingly common (especially in kittens) and will require immediate veterinary attention.

Dogs with long floppy ears (such as cocker spaniels, labradors and golden retrievers) are at higher risk of ear infections because the ear will trap moisture and warmth, providing a great environment for bacteria and yeast to grow.

Have a close look at the skin on the inside of a dog's ears. If it's smooth and looks normal, then no worries. If it's red and has lots of small raised nodules (like leather), then be a little careful. The recent school of thought is that this may be an early clue to allergies or food sensitivities that will become a bigger problem later in life.

Legs

They should be straight and free of bowing and bends. All joints should flex and extend freely, with no pain when moved. Pay particular attention to the elbows, knees and hips which should be freely moveable without clicking or discomfort. In small dogs, meticulously check the knees. The kneecaps are prone to slipping in and out of joint which will cause lameness, discomfort and early onset of arthritis.

To check for slipping kneecaps (luxating patellas), place your fingers over the front of the knee joint. The small, firm bulge is the kneecap. Keep your fingertips on this as you bend the knee joint back and forth. If the kneecaps are prone to slipping, then they will flick out towards the inside of the leg. The kneecap is most likely to slip when the leg is straightened. So feel for any movement of the kneecap at this phase of the leg bending.

A classic sign of slipping kneecaps is a dog that walks freely and then suddenly turns lame, unable to straighten or bear weight on its leg. When walking and running, the animal should move freely and not limp, favour or hold up any particular leg.

The teeth should be free of discolouration and the breath should be fresh.

The eyes should be clear and bright, and not held closed, weeping or sore.

Breathing and circulation

Your vet is trained to check the heart and lungs for any signs of disease. Heart abnormalities and breathing problems (such as asthma, kennel cough and bronchitis) are hard to detect without significant training and equipment. However, the hallmarks of these conditions can be easily seen. Signs of coughing, sneezing and wheezing should be treated with caution. Breathing should be slow and deep, and an effortless process. It's considered abnormal for most pets to be forced to breathe with their mouths open, with the obvious exception of a panting dog.

Chest

The ribcage should be rounded and breathing shouldn't be an obvious effort. When feeling the ribs, they should have a definite spring and elasticity to them, much like bed springs. Check to see that while no ribs can be seen, each rib can be felt when you run your fingers along the ribcage. This is a sign that the animal is at the right weight.

Belly

Depending on how recent and how large the last feed was, the belly should be a smooth continuation of the chest with no dramatic changes in width. No obvious bulges or lumps should be present. Make a special check down the middle of the belly to ensure there are no signs of hernias. An umbilical hernia is the most common type and is usually a soft swelling (about the size of a grape) just underneath the skin at the spot where their 'belly button' is. They can be easily corrected with surgery at the time of desexing to eliminate the risk of the hernia enlarging and becoming life-threatening. Also, a bulging belly is not a sign of good health as many people may think. Certainly it may point to a good appetite, however, large numbers of worms will cause this appearance in some animals.

Feel all over the legs for any sore spots, paying special attention to the joints.

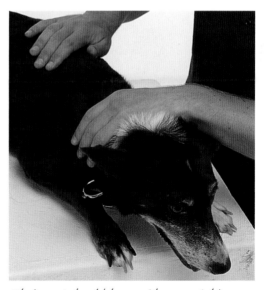

Their coat should have a 'showroom' shine and be free of any evidence of fleas.

Coat

The coat should be clean and have a shine present. The hair should not feel greasy or dry. Check for the nasties like fleas and lice. Fleas can live anywhere on the body, but typically target the area above the base of the tail. Hairless patches may have become that way through excess scratching and irritation. Try not to use the amount of hair being shed in a young animal as a guide to how much will be shed when the animal is mature. The short, fine coat of a youngster is usually quite different to the longer, more durable covering that grows through in later life.

Skin

The skin is visible on the hairless areas of the belly and when the hair is parted. Check the skin for any dry, scaly patches, or an oily feel. The actual colour of the skin depends on the type of the animal and the amount of pigment. Lumps or bumps should all be checked out by a vet, while pimples and welts may indicate anything from a mite infestation through to a bacterial infection or an allergy.

Be wary of young kittens that have scaly, hairless patches of skin. These may be ringworm.

Ringworm is actually a fungal infection of the skin and coat, rather than another wriggly parasite. It's certainly treatable, but the infection can also be transferred to you, causing some unsightly skin irritations in rather obvious areas.

The backend

Any recent history of diarrhoea in a pet is easily seen with a hopefully not-so-close inspection of the rear end. Diarrhoea may occur from time to time with no significant or worrying cause, but it could be a sign of a dietary sensitivity or food allergy that may be a lifelong problem. Redness around the anus should arouse suspicion of either recurrent diarrhoea, worms, constipation or impacted anal glands.

> *TIP*
> *Use the ribs to check if your pet is in a healthy weight range. If you can feel each rib, but not see each one when they stand, then you're probably right on the money.*

It pays to be wary of overly-quiet pets.

Lively pets that settle are a good choice.

Pet profiling

Can you predict an adult animal's personality by watching it as a 6 week old? Well, it's a bit of a risky business as there are so many influences on a pet's natural personality as it grows up, that could make it sociable and gregarious as opposed to being timid and reserved. Having said that, it's handy to look out for personality traits and what they might indicate.

If the potential pet is quiet and withdrawn from other animals

The animal may be either naturally shy and not overly energetic, or possibly sick and physically depressed. Be wary of these sorts of animals, as they may actually be that way due to a medical reason. Mention their quiet state to the supplier.

In a pound situation, where the animals are often fully grown or close to maturity, this level of calmness may be a desirable quality, provided that the vet has given the health tick of approval.

These types of animals are especially suitable for people with small yards or those in apartments.

If the potential pet has a mix of quiet and energetic times

This is usually the most desirable mix. These animals display the physical capability to play and be lively, but at the same time, have a personality that can settle when it needs to.

If the potential pet has a never-ending energy supply

This type will be loads of fun and likely to be a laugh-a-minute. This energy shows that they are likely to be in good health and mobile if they can keep up this sort of pace for long periods. The only concern here would be that they could be too 'in your face' and may become obsessive in their need for human company. This may be an issue for those people that work long hours, or are unable to physically play with their animal.

125

This pet profile type is the most breed-dependent. In dogs that aren't naturally anxious or prone to barking (such as cavaliers, shih tzus, whippets and greyhounds) this will be a desirable character type as it is unlikely to ever 'bubble over' into undesirable behaviour. For those dogs that are already a little prone to over-exuberance, like terriers, it may be an unwelcome character trait. In these breeds, it may be more prudent to go with a quieter puppy.

The shaking dog

If you encounter a puppy that looks like you would if you were wearing nothing but shorts in the Antarctic, then take note of it. It could certainly be cold, but that shivering is usually an indication of anxiety. It's common in the small, white, fluffy brigade (bichon frise, maltese, poodle and so on), but almost all breeds can show it. These dogs tend to be needy and can suffer from separation anxiety. They will often tell the world of their worries by barking, or be destructive by chewing or digging.

> **TIP**
>
> As a general rule when choosing a puppy, try to avoid the most exuberant and domineering puppies, but also steer clear of the shy and withdrawn ones. Something in the middle usually makes the best pet.

Putting the bite on

All kittens and puppies will 'mouth' and 'play-bite' between the ages of about 2–6 months while they are teething. This stimulates the new adult teeth to develop and replace the little razor blade teeth that are already there. Mouthing is quite normal. Actual bites with a definite lunge are not. While it is possible to train this out of a dog or cat, seeing this behaviour in a young animal should provide some deterrent to you taking it home. Especially if that small biting bundle of fluff has big plans growthwise, or belongs to a breed where some aggression is reported. The most accurate profiling is performed on fully grown animals. The parents of the pet you're after always gives clues as to what you can expect.

Ain't nothing like a pound dog

What you see is usually what you get in these cases. A barking, hyperactive dog is likely to stay that way and may prove unsuitable for small yards and apartments. A dog that can seem relaxed and quiet in an environment full of other animals and abundant noise will usually find the peace and quiet of a home a breeze. These dogs could make great pets for those people that lead busy lives, or even the elderly.

The best way to assess a fully grown dog in a shelter or pound situation is to first watch its response when you approach it. Some excitement is obviously good and points to an affectionate animal, but uncontrollable amounts may prove difficult to contain later in life. When the dog is returned to its enclosure, walk away, out of its sight, and wait there. A dog that seems disappointed but settles should make a fairly dependable but relaxed companion. Those that are distressed and bark, scratch, or try to dig, will

certainly be your best mate should you take them home, but will often expect company 24/7 and will voice their disapproval should they not get it.

Remember though, that animals in a pound or shelter are under large amounts of stress and understandably feel lonely and isolated, which amplifies their all-important character traits.

In sickness or in health?

Without five years of veterinary training and lacking those essential elements of a vet's medical bag — the stethoscope and the ice-cold thermometer — I don't expect you to be able to know for sure whether a pet is in sickness or in health. But, knowing the nuances of the most common nasties will help you steer clear of the pets with them, and the people selling them. If you are able to detect the slightest hint of these, you'll be way ahead of the rest, and might just earn yourself an honorary thermometer.

Cat flu

Reckon you look bad with a case of the flu? Your cat will put you to shame in the sneezing, coughing and snot department if it ever gets a bout of cat flu. Cat flu is caused by a viral infection of the upper respiratory tract (nose, throat, mouth, and even eyes). It is caused by two viruses, feline calicivirus and feline herpesvirus, and is extremely contagious to other cats.

A kitten with cat flu will sneeze, cough, have a runny nose (often green), have weepy eyes and be quiet, withdrawn and not interested in food.

A playful cat is likely to be a healthy cat. Be wary of those animals that appear to be depressed and lethargic.

127

A closer check can show some ulcers on the tongue and a high temperature, indicating a fever. So what can be done? Each vaccination a kitten receives contains some protection against these viruses. These shots won't prevent your cat from getting cat flu, but they will make it look more like a cold, rather than a potentially fatal flu. Antibiotics and nursing care (feeding, giving water) will help a cat through it most of the time. If you ever board your cat in a cattery, make sure that your cat, and those around it, have been fully vaccinated.

Unlike our flu virus, once a cat gets cat flu, the virus never truly leaves its body. Instead, it will sit there and wait until the cat is under the weather before it causes another bout of the sickness. Over a lifetime it can be a really unpleasant (and costly) health problem. In unvaccinated cats, and those that aren't 100 per cent vaccinated, it can be fatal. So in your search for a pet cat, look out for the trademark signs. A person selling a cat can wipe away most of the evidence before you see it, but be suspicious if the cat's eyes aren't fully open, there is any sneezing or coughing, or if the cat seems quiet.

If you see a cat with what looks like cat flu, don't buy it. If you have bought a cat with cat flu, inform the breeder, pound or pet store. If you wish to keep it, get veterinary attention as soon as you can. The quicker it's treated, the less long-term hassles you will have.

Chlamydia

Chlamydia is the other cause of the snuffles in kittens. But before you start asking serious questions about where your cat has been, and what has it been up to (and before you start looking through your cat's little black book), let me just say, it's a different type of chlamydia. It looks similar to cat flu, with the eyes and nose most affected. You'll see weepy, sore and red eyes, and often a runny nose as well. This infection is treatable with a specific antibiotic.

Guilty conscience? Be very afraid if you smell something strong coming from the lounge room — and a look like this coming from your dog.

Diarrhoea

If you haven't experienced a really impressive case of bad diarrhoea in a young pet, you haven't lived. Unlike many other conditions, it's easy to detect — you'll usually see it reserved for the more special rooms of the house, but amazingly, the smell will find its way into all rooms. But is it always serious and what causes it?

Diarrhoea is basically the body's way of trying to get rid of something that it doesn't want. The theory is, the quicker it comes out, the better.

Should you avoid pets that have signs of diarrhoea? It really depends on the actual cause.

Those worth noting are:

Parvovirus The word that sends a chill down dog owners' spines. It's extremely nasty and often fatal, but puppy vaccinations prevent it occurring. It causes an almost explosive and uncontrollable bloody and smelly diarrhoea. If you see an unvaccinated pup with bad diarrhoea, avoid it like the plague.

129

Coronavirus This virus causes a watery-brown river of diarrhoea from your dog. Not usually fatal but will knock your pup around for quite a while. You can actually vaccinate against this now, which can only be a good thing.

Feline Infectious Enteritis A really serious virus in cats, although it can be difficult to pick from other causes of diarrhoea. Cats will look depressed, go off their food and have vomiting, as well as diarrhoea. My advice would be to just walk away from there.

Worms It's a pretty safe bet that all young pets have worms at some stage. They will pick them up from their mother, litter-mates or the world around them. All worms can cause a mucousy, often blood-spotted, diarrhoea. In the case of tapeworms, you will even see them in the faeces — they look like small grains of rice that wriggle. You can often pick a wormy pet by the way they have a big fat belly, but are skinny everywhere else, have a dry, harsh coat and have a really strong appetite, but still don't grow well. Wormy pets will usually recover if given regular de-worming, but some effects, such as stunted growth, may remain if the worm problem was severe enough.

Gastroenteritis Worthy of note, because there tends to be action at both ends — vomiting and diarrhoea. Usually caused by either eating the wrong thing (like the neighbour's curry takeaway out of their garbage bin), or by a stomach bug. Without a vet's examination, it can be indistinguishable from more serious viruses, or digestive system conditions.

Overeating Probably the most common cause of diarrhoea in young animals. A young pet's body is small, but their appetites are large. And just like at an all-you-can eat buffet, it's amazing just how much you can fit in when you try. The only problem is that the little gut of a young pet can only digest a certain amount — the rest gets fast-tracked out of there. You can usually pick this type of diarrhoea by its pasty consistency; it's not watery or bloody, but it hits new levels on the smell-o-meter.

Change of diet The gut of a pet is a little boring — it doesn't like change. Switch a pet to a new food and chances are that the little one's stomach will voice its disapproval with some pasty diarrhoea. Once again, there shouldn't be any blood or big signs of sickness, so this type of diarrhoea isn't a massive concern apart from the inconvenience. This is a more common issue when you get a pet home, than when it's at a breeder, pet store or pound.

If you do want to change the diet of a pet, do it over four days; time enough for the gut to adjust to the change. Here's how:

- Day 1: ¾ old food, ¼ new food
- Day 2: ½ old food, ½ new food
- Day 3: ¼ old food, ¾ new food
- Day 4: all new food

Sad eyes

Young puppies and kittens don't cry nearly as much as their human baby counterparts, yet many have big clumps of gunk that form under their eyes, as if they have been getting a little emotional without any tissues close by. This is usually a sign of having blocked tear ducts. The tear duct is basically a long tube, like an enclosed water slide, that takes tears from the eye for a ride down to empty out into the nostrils. We also have them, which is why we get all sniffly when we cry. However, like a trouble-maker does at a water park, a blockage in that water slide spells trouble. Nothing can pass down the tube and, like a group of disgruntled kids, all those tears pool at the top, resulting in a big clump of goo in the corner of the eye.

You can get blockages for a number of reasons. As an animal grows, the tube is open for business some days and closed on others, however, when fully grown it should remain open.

Emotional? Or is it really blocked tear ducts?

What can block it up is infection. When a young fluffball gets a viral or bacterial infection, everything becomes swollen and there are a lot of bugs around. Cat flu and chlamydia often cause this in cats, while for dogs, it's often those that are prone to eye irritations caused by allergies or infection that are affected. These issues can keep the tube closed for good, unless the tube is flushed by a vet.

So if the pet you're looking at has 'sad eyes', it could be due to blocked tear ducts. They can be fixed (at least for a while), but be aware of what might be causing it in the first place.

It could be a clue to a kitten that may have cat flu or a dog that has allergies, so be wary of those emotional eyes and what they might be hiding.

WELCOME HOME

Bringing your new pet home for the first time is about as exciting as it gets. It's where that pet becomes a part of your family. And just like when you are first invited into a friend's house, it's good to try and make a good first impression. Piles of rubbish, scurrying cockroaches and levels of noise comparable to a music festival may not be the way to welcome that someone special. A clean, dry and organised pad is the way to go. You want to be prepared for anything from day one. Their sleeping area and bed should be in place and their food and water bowls should be set out. For cats, and those animals to be toilet-trained onto litter, a litter tray should be placed in an easily accessible, but not easily viewed spot. Remember, they like their privacy too. Keep at least a few feet between their food and their litter tray. Understandably, they like to keep their distance in this department.

How to play it

Expect that they will be dazed, confused and a little anxious when they first arrive. Their world has been turned upside-down, and it's now up to you to let them know that it's going to be okay.

The first step is to keep them inside, preferably in just one or two rooms. Let them get used to you and the surroundings in a low-stress way. Show them where the food and water bowls are.

Don't rush these crucial first stages. Be gentle and let them do everything in their own time. Always use a relaxed and reassuring tone, and

Dog tired? Keeping up with the constant energy and excitement of kids can be a challenge for any pup.

praise them freely. You are there to be trusted and certainly not feared. Imagine yourself in a foreign land — you don't know how you got there, you don't know a soul and you don't understand a word they say. Just as you would be, your pet will be looking for someone to depend upon. These first few moments should be just between you and your pet. Even though friends and neighbours might want to be a part of it, crowding will only confuse your little mate.

Your home isn't 'boot camp', so leave all the training until after you have both become accustomed to each other. It might help to have low expectations for toilet training on these first few days — putting the business in the right place seems to have a low priority initially.

These first days are often not without the odd whimper or crying episode. In the cases where a few toys, a comforting hot water bottle or even a ticking clock (which mimics mum's heartbeat) don't help, there is a big urge to 'mother' your pup or kitten by cuddling your pet to sleep. However, this may be a short-term solution that causes long-term problems. They will often expect constant affection and even whine as a way of getting attention in the first place. Try to realise that whimpering, even if a little hard to watch, is a normal part of them growing up.

Kids ... meet the pet

This might come as a surprise to many, but even though children are smaller than adults, our pets are often far more intimidated and fearful of them. But why is that?

It comes down to the fact that adults are predictable. We walk a certain way, we talk a certain way and it rarely changes. We do few unexpected things. Kids, however, are a bit of a lottery. It's what makes them so unique. Some talk, others garble, some even scream. Their movements are unscripted — they may crawl or walk and they fall about. And in the middle of it all, a little fluff ball, no bigger than a toddler's stuffed toy, sits and waits — always with one eye on the erratic mini-adult.

It's to be expected that your children will want to be all over your new pet. And it's great for them to play a big role in its life, and they will, but slowly. Now you know how a pet sees a child, you can realise how crucial the introduction is. Your pet must see your house as a refuge from the outside world, not a world turned inside-out.

Teach your children to be gentle and play softly around the new pet. When it is time to meet, they should get down to the pet's height and gently call him or her in a soft tone. Try to let the pet come to them, that way there's no risk of scaring it off. Teaching them to hold their hand outstretched with a treat is a good initial peace offering, and can add some encouragement to a play session.

Pets are not toys and, unlike some kids, can't play all day everyday. They need their quiet time and should always be left alone when they are sleeping or eating.

How to hold a pet

The basics of holding a pet like a puppy, kitten, rabbit, guinea pig or mouse are all the same. It's all about support and being gentle. Pets will only struggle when they are scared or they don't feel secure. Always teach kids to use two hands. One should hold the chest between the front legs while the other hand should support the back half by holding around the belly and the hips. Once they have the pet in both hands, they

The right way to hold a nervous bunny.

should gently move it in to be held securely against their chest, but not too tightly. This feeling of being held snugly, should help to relax a pet.

There is always the risk of the pet struggling free and falling. For that reason, teach your child how to hold the pet when they are sitting down. That way, any escape attempts won't end in disaster. Only when they are skilled in holding should they be allowed to stand and hold. Remember, a pet should never be picked up by its leg or its tail.

Luckily, pets that are good with children (like those featured in The Best Beasts section) often understand their role in this situation. For those pets, it's often best for them to be tolerant and go limp than fight the inevitable. They are going to be held whether they like it or not.

Holding birds, however, is entirely different. They simply don't like being held and any unnecessary stress can kill them. So watch them, but try not to touch them or make sudden

On the lookout for the next group of friends.

Where they sleep

It seemed like not so long ago the question was: do we let the pet sleep inside or make it sleep outside? But somewhere along the line a shift occurred. Now the question has become: do they sleep in the bed or just out of it? While casually chatting to my clients I am always amazed at how many of them share the bed with their dog or cat. In fact, I know of husbands who, night after night, are pushed slowly to the edge of the mattress and forced to stand their ground in the face of a blanket-stealing, pillow-dribbling dog that lies fully outstretched. But, should it be this way?

Obviously we are all individual in how we see our pets. Some are seen more like furry little people that deserve all rights and privileges, while others are, well, just referred to as 'the dog' or 'the cat'. Where we choose as a place for our pets to sleep is often a reflection of this. In reality, the best place for a pet to sleep is where both parties are happy for it to sleep.

If this is outside, then it should be given a clean, dry bed with some sort of blanket or rug for comfort and warmth. This is especially important for short-coated dogs and short-haired cats that may not have been bred for cool conditions. The bed should be raised off the ground and the bedding washed regularly to remove dirt and any other nasties like fleas or flea eggs that may be picked up. A few pet-safe toys in the bed as well may occupy the animal enough so that digging or barking (often due to boredom) is not seen as such a good idea on those long, lonely nights.

If your pet is going to sleep inside, find a good place and try to stick with it. The laundry may be ideal as you are able to have their food and water close by, and any dog- or cat-like smells won't cause an issue. A pet bed is still a good idea, as it

movements around them. If you do ever need to hold them, remember they can't be held too tightly as this will suffocate them. They should be held in a loose towel for short periods. If you want to be a bird expert, there is a way of holding them that means they can still breathe freely. Ask your vet about this.

The new pet will need to get used to your own children well before it's ready to meet your kids' friends. If your kids are good enough to handle your pet carefully, then they will make good instructors for teaching their friends how to behave around their pet. Encouraging them to take responsibility for their new little brother or sister has many benefits — most notably, for the pet itself.

Restless sleeper. A new pup will take some time adjusting to their new surroundings.

will raise the animal off the floor, make the animal more inclined to settle at night, and decrease the risk of any pressure sores occurring.

If you want your pet to sleep inside and in the bed, my main advice is to be careful. This is sending a fairly strong message that your pet is entitled to be more human than animal. You must be clear at setting strong boundaries about what they can and cannot do. They must always be invited to jump onto the bed, and must always jump off the bed when told. You should always be seen to be in charge.

The inside word on being inside

There is a big temptation with a new pet to 'mother' it by constantly lavishing affection on it, cuddling it whenever it whimpers and letting it sleep in your bed while it gets used to its new house. This may comfort your little friend in the short term and will often lessen the whining. Long term though, what you will create is a dependent pet. As typically, if you do something for long enough, your pet will get used to it. They

will expect attention day and night and may even whine, whimper or bark as a way of gaining affection in the first place. Being out of the house during the day for work may prove difficult to handle. You may be better off doing the hard yards initially, and have your little mate sleep away from the bedroom and your company. Realising that a bit of whimpering is almost to be expected, even if it is difficult to watch and does tug at the heartstrings, it will probably prove to be a happier solution for everyone in the long run.

Things don't always go to plan, so you have to be ready to adapt and find new solutions — provided they are workable. Take Rosie for example. Born in a cold and damp hollow log on the outskirts of a small rural town, a move to the warmth of the coast should have been an easy adaptation. You'd be entitled to think that the five-star warmth of a foam bed, topped with a woollen blanket, with a complimentary mini-bar service of puppy food and water as well as a talkback radio station on low volume, would seem irresistible to a country kid not used to these city comforts. Even a frosted heat lamp was used to provide some extra warmth and ensure that there was no fear of the dark. How wrong could one family — with two vets on staff — be? Quite wrong is the answer. The fact that the whimpering was present even while we were playing with Rosie in her new room was a bad sign — it merely continued unabated when we left her to 'sleep'. It was obvious that it wasn't our company that little Rosie was missing, nor was it due to a complaint over the service provided to her. Instead it was the location. This was certainly not the farm and this room was certainly not the hollow log. The closest we could provide was the outdoor undercover area that jutted out from the dining room. So out went the blankets and the food, and we all gave this a try. The moment the blackness of night leached all the colour from her stumpy body, so too did it draw away her sadness. For immediately, all was still and quiet at Scenic Drive. And it remained so from that moment on — the country girl preferred her country comforts.

What makes a good bed?
Rosie recommends for dogs

A raised hessian bed with a strong steel frame is hard to beat for any canine. Having it off the ground makes the entry onto the bed and the exit so much easier and prevents the bed picking up any moisture. Throw in a few washable blankets and it's a low cost, high comfort choice.

All the flash, new dog beds seem to be pretty close to the mark. Provided you can get them off the ground and ensure they are washable. They vary in colour, design and size which should hopefully ensure that your supposedly tough farm dog isn't crashing out on a chihuahua-designed, velour cushion the size of a postage stamp.

Many a night has been spent on this tried and true bed, and it's still going strong. A fresh blanket atop makes it as good as new.

137

Poo-Cat recommends for cats

Just as in dogs, hundreds of new styles of cat beds are flooding the market. Comfort is obviously important but washability is paramount. After all, as Poo-Cat will attest, accidents do happen — even if you aren't truly responsible for them.

The funny thing about cats is that, being fully in control of their own destiny, they may choose a warm car bonnet over a luxurious hand-stitched, down-feather bed. A few blankets or towels in a suitable spot are also fancied by the felines. If you want a cheap, easy and comfortable alternative, don't do what Poo-Cat did — instead, use the litter tray. A large rectangular plastic tray (with a blanket or soft towel as a mattress) can be a surprise favourite. An average-sized cat will fit in there comfortably and the raised sides seem to provide some degree of contentment and comfort.

TIPS FOR THE FIRST WEEK

Once they have settled in, most puppies and kittens waste no time in making themselves at home. They may even take certain liberties in their new surroundings. How much they leave their mark on your home can be the source of some degree of amazement and perhaps even some frustration. Most of these little glitches around the home are the result of either an instinctive urge gone wrong, or just plain boredom on the part of our little mates. So let's look at how you put the brakes on these four-legged tenants before you end up in the doghouse yourself.

Chewing

Not even the most optimistic or determined new pet owner will stop a puppy or kitten chewing. This is because chewing is a normal process brought on by teething; where the baby teeth are replaced by the adult teeth. Instead, what you should be aiming for is to control the chewing and redirect it away from your furniture to more suitable objects.

So, provide some viable alternatives to your limbs and the furniture. Chew toys like rubber 'kongs', rope toys or squeaky toys are all attractive to a youngster. Make it clear which areas aren't for munching on.

If they bite onto you, act immediately and say a firm 'no' while looking directly into their eyes. The pup or kitten should then be taken away to sit by itself in a 'sin-bin' area (a quiet room or laundry). Leave it there for at least 10 minutes before inviting it to return. Any repeat infringement earns another stint in the sin bin.

If they chew the furniture, you must catch them in the act for any lesson to be learned. Once

A young man making his mark on the world.

again say a firm 'no', pick them up and place them in a designated sin bin area. If this persists, you may try citronella oil as a deterrent for dogs or wrap a temporary protective covering over the areas for cats. Try to be tolerant as teething won't last forever, and things should settle down after 6 months of age.

Barking

Barking is certainly one of the ways a dog communicates. Knowing what they're trying to say is the real art though. Bored dogs will bark when they are left alone and have nothing to interest their active minds. They often pine for human company. So, provide some entertainment for them. Uncooked bones and a few toys help — also leaving a radio on will make the house seem less empty.

It also helps to make them less dependent on you. Don't make a big scene when you leave for work. This only alerts them to the fact you will be gone for at least 8 hours. Instead, slip out quietly without so much as a 'goodbye'. If the problem persists, then a citronella collar can help to train them out of barking. Ask your vet about this.

Excited dogs will bark when something they see or hear is of interest to them. The best way to manage this is to continually re-expose them to the sound until they become so used to it, they are desensitised. A ringing doorbell is a common example of noise that may interest a dog.

Whatever you do, don't respond to their barking with barking of your own — yelling at them only encourages them to bark more.

Escaping

Some dogs have the capacity to make Houdini look like Who-dini — their escape artistry is that good. Pets will escape if they are bored or frightened. The most common times for dogs to escape is either when their owners are at work or during thunderstorms and fireworks displays. Anticipating the latter and moving the dog inside is always a good move. Besides this, ensure your fences are in good condition and your gates are self-closing (see the earlier section on Fencing).

Always ensure your pet has a microchip and a name tag (with phone numbers) as even the best designed fortress won't hold some dogs.

Crying at night

This seems to tug at every maternal or paternal instinct you have, and even some you didn't realise you had. Young puppies and kittens learn from an early age that crying earns attention from mum, and considering all the changes they go

Scratching

Many a good couch, or even a human limb, has earned that 'frayed' look by kitty's sharp claws. However, you shouldn't forget that scratching is a natural behaviour that helps them mark their territory as well as keep their claws healthy. So we need to find a way to lessen the damage from scratching while transferring it to a more suitable location.

The first step is to trim your cat's nails. Get your local vet to show you how the first time. Next, introduce your cat to a scratching post. This is basically a wooden post covered in carpet or rope that can be used as a sacrifice to be scratched to your cat's desire. Let your cat get used to the post before slowly moving it away from the sofa you are trying to save. You can encourage your cat to use the scratching post by placing a few cat biscuits on the post, or by rubbing some catnip into the fabric of the scratching post.

Toilet training

Toilet training should be a lot simpler than people make it. The key is being able to anticipate when the plumbing is going to kick into action and build a routine around this. Know that accidents will happen and that the process will take weeks to truly show results.

A dog or cat will have an urge to go to the toilet when it wakes up after a sleep, and after a meal or a drink. So at these times, escort your animal to a designated 'drop-zone'. For puppies, this may be a corner of the garden, while for kittens it's often a litter tray.

Wait patiently while your pet composes themselves. They may take some time to produce, but be patient and let them relax. When they

Like a tiger! Scratching is a natural behaviour in cats.

through in your first few days together, it's no surprise that you will hear the odd whimper. How you respond to it is very important. If you have provided them with a warm bed (a hot water bottle will help — but ensure it's not too hot) and they have been fed and taken to the toilet, then it should really be time for them to sleep. Say goodnight to them and go to bed. As hard as it is, any whimpering from that point on should be ignored — for cuddling them and letting them sleep in your bed will only encourage more whining and crying from then on. On a different night, you can see how they settle with the light on or off (they may be scared of the dark) and even let them sleep with an article of clothing with your smell on it.

'It was him!'. Toilet training isn't always an instant success and accidents do happen.

finally go, praise them excitedly and even offer a food reward. Be persistent — it will take weeks for them to get it right, but eventually the routine will become second nature.

If you want to take toilet etiquette to new levels then you can even teach your pet the 'wee' command. This is simply a matter of saying 'wee' as your pet is urinating and praising with pats and food rewards when he or she has finished. Over time, they will begin to associate the word 'wee' with the act. Just be careful if you happen to be telling a story over dinner about what 'We got up to over the weekend', and the dog is close by.

GATHERING THE TROOPS

So the house is prepared, the troops have been briefed and all resources are at the ready, just waiting to be called into action. But all is quiet. A calm has descended upon the expectant and excited household. The hands on the clock slow-march onwards, lapping the circle slowly in defiance, the fridge buzzes impatiently. Something seems to be missing from this scene.

The rattle of the car keys energises the room. Everyone jumps to their feet. It's time to go. That room will never seem so empty again. It's time to get that pet. So let's have a look around …

141

the best beasts

THE CRITERIA

Let's take a look at the best beasts to choose from. I've made it easy for you and selected those pets that I reckon stand tall above the rest. That's not to say that these are the only animals that you should choose from — they merely present the smallest risk. They are tried and true. Reliable pets that don't take themselves and their needs too seriously, but at the same time believe in giving you back bucketloads of fun and affection for the value you place in them. There are a few surprises coming up, and a few animals that you wouldn't have thought of owning before. So let's drop in on each of them, one at a time. To help you choose a little (or not so little) mate, I've rated some important factors to consider, from zero (☆) to five stars (★★★★★). So look at where you live, what you can and cannot do and what you want in a pet. How they look is only a small part of what makes them a suitable pet. And I've explained their importance below. Take each consideration seriously and take your time making your choice — this is a long-term commitment. Chances are that the pet you choose will be around longer than 10 fashion trends, you'll move house around them, go on holidays and change jobs — in short, they will see all of your ups and downs. Among all this, they can be the one constant, reliable companion in your life. All they ask is that you be understanding of their needs. So choose smartly and take time to consider the important criteria.

TIME Ask yourself: do you have the time to not only do the basics with your pet, but also keep it happy with one-on-one attention and exercise? If you're working long hours, then a high-maintenance pet is not the ideal choice for you. Choose a pet whose need for time suits your ability to provide it.

SPACE The amount of space you have available can be negated to a certain extent by the amount of time you have available to put in to your pet. Having said that, things will run more smoothly if you work with your space. Fish, birds, rabbits, guinea pigs and cats may be more suited to apartments, than, for example, a farm-bred border collie. But each pet is unique in terms of its requirements for space. This is especially the case in dogs where small size doesn't always mean small space. The terrier group of dogs as well as the maltese, were bred to be hunters and are instinctively hyperactive dogs. Meanwhile, gentle giants like great danes and greyhounds are 90 per cent relaxation, 10 per cent perspiration, and will kick back and relax if they need to.

COST Pets are certainly the gift that keeps on giving — but the cost of all that giving can add up. There is the initial price of a pet along with the set-up costs (bed, food, bowls, filters, and so on). Where you can get really stung is in the ongoing costs. Routine vet bills and food will add up. Then there is always the unforeseen risk of a major injury or illness that is often expensive. As a general rule (once you have gone through all the initial set-up), the larger the animal, the more expensive it will be. They eat more and their medication is usually more expensive. I am of the belief that if you take on a pet as your best friend, then it is your duty to see them through sickness and health. So you need to be prepared.

As an example, for a large dog such as a labrador, by 6 months of age, the least you can have expected to pay is $180 for vaccinations, $30 for worming, $70 for heartworm prevention and around $200 for desexing. Food will add another $120. Leashes, collars, beds and food bowls top it up by another $100. So for a totally healthy labrador to celebrate its half birthday you will be down at least $700. This doesn't include the cost of buying the dog, and doesn't take into account the fact that one or two sniffles and sick days are common.

EXERCISE Some pets love the easy-going life we provide to them, while for other pets it goes against every urge they know. Some animals, like fish, even take care of it all themselves. A reasonable amount of exercise will not only satisfy the appetites of those that want to feel the wind in their hair, but it will also make pets happier and healthier. Some pets require a surprisingly small amount of exercise, while others have all the endurance and drive of a marathon runner. Knowing which pet needs what, will mean you make the right decision about the pet that best fits in with you, as after all, they can't (usually) exercise themselves. And remember, they might not be the only one that feels better after a run.

KIDS Your goal should be to have a pet that enriches your children's lives and mixes so well with the kids that it becomes an integral and valued member of the family. For this to happen a pet must know its place in terms of seniority — they must be on the bottom rung of the ladder. Even toddlers that may be the same size or smaller than the pet must be that animal's master. This 'pecking order' is controlled by how you and your children treat your pet. You must let it know its place. Some pets slip into this role with ease, happy to just roll with the punches and even watch over and care for the kids. Others take some convincing.

NOISE If I was a vindictive person and wanted to really annoy my neighbours, I would ship-in a truckload of roosters and position them in a pen just outside my neighbour's bedroom window. But I'm not and you shouldn't try it. I've seen it done and it's not the nicest thing. Instead, you should buy your pet with at least some consideration for the neighbours. A barking dog, an aggressive, urine-spraying cat, or a screeching bird, will only alienate you from the people you should be friendly with. And if you want to look at it from a personal perspective, that offensive urine smell and the incessant barking might just get to you too. Some types of pets are prone to making their feelings known, be it out of frustration, boredom or anxiety. In suburban or inner city areas, space is at a premium, and where your dog sleeps may be just feet away from where your neighbour sleeps. So if you live in one of these areas, love thy neighbour and bear in mind their need for peace and quiet. Even though the amount of noise produced is heavily influenced by other factors, such as the time (or the lack of time) spent with your pets, their environment and what other options to noise-making are available, some breeds will stamp their noisiness more than the adolescent neighbour that's just been given a drum kit for Christmas.

LIFESPAN No-one really likes to think about how long they might have with their pets, and the best approach is always going to be to live everyday to the full. Where it is important though, is when you need to match your pet's lifespan to your life-stage. A long-lived animal (like a dog or cat) bought for a teenager, will usually find itself under the care of mum and dad by the time it hits the turbulent teenage years itself. Long-living pets will obviously become a bigger part of your family, but the dependence goes both ways. You need to plan a large portion of your life around them, and they will typically require more help as the years roll by. Short-lived pets may be better for those people unsure about how truly prepared they are for a pet and for when you are looking to try out the whole 'pet concept' where kids are concerned. These short-lived animals may act as a good 'test pet' to see if a stronger commitment (to say a dog) is likely to work.

⭐ **GROOMING** We all need a bit of work to look our best. And just like us, some pets need more than others. However, grooming can be a time-consuming exercise, as well as an expensive one. Whether you want your pet to look its best or to just to look like a pet is up to you. The fact is that some pets need grooming more than others and many of these need it not only to look good but also to avoid medical problems like hairballs, knots, dermatitis, heat-stress and infections.

⭐ **PERSONALITY** How much do they give back? The world of pets really has it all in terms of personality. At one end of the scale are your pet rocks, right through to your extraverted, in your face 'look at me' sort of companion. Some pets are super-cool and make you work for any affection, while others provide an unending supply. Remember that how you involve it with your family and friends will certainly have a big influence. From my experience as a vet the animals that are overflowing with personality and endear themselves to you quickly often become a bigger part of the family, but can be a little more demanding of your time and affection. While those that live the quiet life tend to be a little less 'needy'. So there are positives and negatives to that personality which lies within. While there's no sure way of predicting an individual pet's personality, it's fair to say that some breeds and types are bursting with character while others simply enjoy the quiet life.

Other considerations

Male or female? No sex stands out as making a better pet. They each have their advantages and disadvantages. Males are often more spirited and can be more extraverted and inclined to play, but this exuberance can turn itself into behavioural problems. Females tend to be more gentle and are probably better around kids. However, if treated too firmly, they are prone to becoming a little withdrawn and introverted at times.

Bless this mess? A pet won't simply stay in its own space — they love nothing more than making your house, their house. So when you consider how much time a pet will take up, remember the extra effort of removing their calling cards. Dogs that slobber will have you wiping down the walls daily. Hair will be shed in large quantities by both dogs and cats, and the youthful stage can leave your carpet bearing the unpleasant scars of toilet training and gut upsets. The teething period will also leave its own unique finish to the legs of your chairs and tables. It's all part of owning an animal, so see it as part of the experience.

Young or old pet? We are inevitably drawn to wanting a young puppy or kitten. They are obviously at their most vulnerable and dependent stage, which is part of the appeal. However, if you don't have the time to be the nanny for these crucial first few months, or are looking to give an old pet a second chance, then a mature pet could be an option. The trick is to choose carefully. A 'mature' animal is surrendered for a reason. Some have ended-up without a home when their owner has passed away, or when they have headed overseas — these can be safe choices. Others are in pounds or animal shelters because of serious behavioural problems and these represent a big risk. See if you can find out the story behind the animal — it will not only save you a lot of hassle, but could also allow you to know each other a little better.

Purebred or mixed breed? The new trend has been towards crossbreeds like labradoodles, spoodles, la schnoodles, spanadors, and whatever else will produce a strange name. Crossbreeding is designed to reduce the incidence of genetic or inherited diseases, as combining two different sets of genes decreases the risk of problems in one breed being passed onto the offspring. Crossbreeds may grow faster and larger than their mixed parents. This effect of crossbreeding is called 'hybrid vigour' and is the result of getting the best from both breeds. Remember that crossing two breeds isn't a guarantee that the offspring will be healthy. What makes up the combination is the important thing. For example, if you cross a dog with bad hips with another dog with bad hips, then the puppies are at a high risk of having, you guessed it, bad hips. The same goes for personality. Bad tempered parents will tend to produce equally bad tempered puppies and kittens. The established crosses have become well known because they have typically produced healthy and well-mannered pups and kittens.

There will always be a place for purebreds. You certainly have a greater idea of what you are getting, which obviously has its appeals, however, having the official papers and a pedigree isn't the be all and end all.

DOGS

If you've ever been overwhelmed by the variety of dogs, don't despair. There's a good reason why you feel this way. You see, across the whole of nature, the dog is one of the most diverse and variable species on the planet. Just think about it. No other species range in size like the dog does. From a tiny chihuahua that can weigh only 1 kg (2 lb) right up to a massive great dane that can top 80 kg (180 lb), the variation is huge.

So with so much variety out there, where do you start? A lot of people have ideas about what size dog they're after. Small dogs tend to win favour with owners wanting more of a 'home-body' dog while the larger breeds have appeal as being more lively and active outdoors-based buddies. But a word of warning on generalising man's best friend. Having a small dog doesn't necessarily mean a small time commitment — the mini breeds are often maxi on their demands of you, whether it be through a need for social interaction, entertainment, exercise or even grooming. On the other hand, it's possible to find a large breed of dog that's more than happy to swap any form of fitness for a futon. The one constant requirement with dogs relates to their great attraction — their personality. They are social creatures; quickly becoming devoted and almost doting on their owners. But please don't make it something that's all one-way traffic. Spend time with them every day, play, interact, and even talk to them. It makes for one big happy family — with the dog at the centre of course.

Confused? Don't be. Use the dogs featured in this section as rock-solid recommendations. There's all sizes, shapes and personalities. And I'm sure you'll find at least one that suits your specifications.

Cavalier King Charles Spaniel

If dogs could throw parties, these guys would insist on being the life of them. They would be the knock-about character, always joking around. Cav's are seemingly always in a good mood and are one of those breeds that genuinely look as though they are smiling when the moment takes them. The only problem with their engaging and endearing personality is that since they will inevitably become everyone's friend, finding some time together might be a bit difficult. Friends of mine that own one always complain that it takes hours to just walk around the block; there are just so many people to say 'hi' to!

The Cav was originally developed from a cross between a King Charles and a cocker spaniel. However, there is really nothing truly regal about this breed. They're a no-nonsense lively and playful companion. Unlike many breeds of a similar size, their temperament is spot-on. They revel in human company, but are rarely unfairly demanding of it. They will bark if strangers are around (and probably then attempt to lick them to death) but aren't a breed renowned for barking unnecessarily, which is one of the great features of them. All of these qualities are reflected in the fact that they are the least-commonly surrendered dog to pounds in Australia, which is quite a rap for them.

Medically speaking, those long floppy ears can cause a few dramas. Once moisture is trapped in there (through swimming, bathing and other activities), it's not getting out in a hurry. So always keep the ears dry to avoid ear infections. The most serious concern with Cav's is associated with their hearts. Heart disease is relatively common, so ensure that your pup and its parents are checked out before you buy. The condition they are most prone to is a mitral valve insufficiency, which your vet will know about — this is where one of the heart valves becomes leaky, affecting the performance of the heart. They aren't a breed that craves loads of exercise, but they love a walk all the same. A good brush every few days should keep their silky coat in order. Remember to keep the hair trimmed in and around the ear canal, and ensure the whole area is kept free of moisture and any wax build-up.

CHEAT NOTES

- For dogs this size, they are one of the best all-round dogs available.

- They are perfect for kids and will become a big part of the family, even being suited to the elderly.

- A good vet check is essential — especially concerning their heart.

- A highly suitable dog for apartment and small space living.

TIME: ★★★ SPACE: ★★ COST: ★★★ EXERCISE: ★★ KIDS: ★★★★★
NOISE: ★★ LIFESPAN: 10–13 years GROOMING: ★★ PERSONALITY: ★★★★

Miniature Schnauzer

The wise old man of the dog world. Looking at them, it's almost expected that some great pearls of wisdom shall be spoken from that moustached mouth that will solve all of life's problems. But in the flesh, these are certainly not dogs that look upon life as one big retirement village — they are an up-and-at-'em adolescent whose facial hair is more of a style choice than a lifestyle statement. They make energetic, enthusiastic little mates that are as dependable as you want them to be. For their size, they are surprisingly brave and will pull their weight as a watchdog, even to the point of watching over the kids. A daily walk is recommended and is even better if it includes a run off the leash to really blow off the cobwebs.

They are pretty robust and healthy on the whole, with just a few niggly little problems (to keep you on your toes of course) that you should look out for in their later years. There is a tendency to develop skin lumps like cysts (which are more of an annoyance than anything else), as well as the occasional skin irritation and allergy. The odd plumbing problem in their urinary tract (due to bladder stones) is also seen. Keeping that moustache at its salt-and-pepper coloured best can require a little work as it often functions as a mop, soaking-up samples of the day's meals. Daily brushing is also recommended (unless you like the shaggy dog look). It is generally an easy care coat, and a stiff-bristled brush is all you should require. Be careful not to overbathe these guys as their skin and coat is prone to drying out a little.

CHEAT NOTES

- *A fun-loving and playful dog whose size doesn't truly reflect their strong personality.*
- *Keeping their unique appearance true to form will take a little work.*
- *Is adaptable to almost all situations — be it an apartment, house or farm, and copes reasonably well with being left alone.*
- *Exercise is always welcomed.*
- *Gets along well with children.*

TIME: ★★★ SPACE: ★★★ COST: ★★★ EXERCISE: ★★★ KIDS: ★★★
NOISE: ★★★ LIFESPAN: 12–14 years GROOMING: ★★★ PERSONALITY: ★★★

Maltese x Shih Tzu

When their eyes met across a crowded dog-kennel, the parents of this crossbreed couldn't have known what their relationship would bring. Their union has brought one of the most popular crossbreeds available today. And fortunately, for the most part, the result brings together the best of both mum and dad while leaving the undesirable parts out of the mix. This so-called 'hybrid-vigour' is what you hope to achieve through crossbreeding. With so many of these dogs around, the problem is not so much finding one, but picking out a healthy and hardy animal. With few breeders specifically producing this cross, it's often up to the pet stores to supply these dogs — so be picky with your pet store, not just with your pet.

Try to realise though, that crossbreeding isn't a fix-all solution to medical or behavioural problems that an animal may have. Certain elements of both breeds still remain in the cross. Some maltese x shih tzus can be a bit of a dentist's delight, with many having an under-bite. When this happens, the teeth don't align properly and the normal act of eating isn't able to keep the tartar away, making them prone to bad teeth and bad breath. Insisting that they eat a high-quality dry food is essential to minimise tartar build-up. Watch out for eye problems caused by blocked tear ducts, or irritation from surrounding hair touching the eyeball. Loose kneecaps and skin allergies are also a concern and should be looked for in the parents.

They tend to be happy little dogs that enjoy exercise but don't demand it. The only thing they can demand is your time and company, so being firm with them and making them less dependent on you is important if they start to show any signs of separation anxiety.

CHEAT NOTES

- Be picky when you choose one. Look at their teeth (in particular, the bite) and eyes.
- Make sure they are well trained — be firm.
- Treat them like a dog and not a person. Stop them getting up on the furniture, the bed, or eating from the table. Give them an inch and they will take a mile and make you pay for it later.
- A daily brush with a stiff brush should take care of the coat. Keeping the hair around the eyes trimmed short is recommended.

TIME: ★★★★ SPACE: ★★ COST: ★★★ EXERCISE: ★★★ KIDS: ★★★
NOISE: ★★★ LIFESPAN: 12–14 years GROOMING: ★★★ PERSONALITY: ★★★

Whippet

Looking like a dog that has been well and truly 'whipped' into shape, the whippet is one of the real 'nice guys' of the dog world. Even though they are nice guys, it's not to say they aren't fast movers — and I'm talking speed here. Just looking at them, it's easy to see that they are descended from the greyhound, and their speed across the ground reflects this. But interestingly, a regular walk and occasional run should be all it takes to satisfy all their exercise needs.

The important thing to understand about whippets is that they are real softies. In a home situation you will be amazed by how gentle, quiet and obedient they are. If anything, they almost take the 'sensitive new age dog' thing too far. They have an overly gentle personality and the way you handle them should reflect this. Being too firm only makes them fret. Sensitive is the key word with these dogs. You must take great care not to allow them to expose their skin to too many extremes. Keeping them indoors in summer may be the only real option, as their thin coat and patchy white skin makes them extremely sensitive to sunburn and skin cancer. But be aware that they can be their own worst enemy here, as their lack of body fat makes them obsessive about sunbaking to keep warm. Winter is also a tough time and many of these dogs need to wear coats as a way of keeping warm. They are also prone to eye diseases like cataracts and PRA (progressive retinal atrophy, an eye disease that causes premature blindness). Despite these medical sensitivities, their gentle and kind personailty makes them a great choice for the family.

CHEAT NOTES

- A sensitive and gentle creature.
- Makes a great pet for kids.
- Suitable for apartments and small houses.
- Has special requirements — needs to avoid temperature extremes and the summer sun.
- An easy coat to care for. An occasional stroke with a glove-brush is all that's required.

TIME: ★★★   SPACE: ★★   COST: ★★★   EXERCISE: ★★★   KIDS: ★★★
NOISE: ★   LIFESPAN: 10-14 years   GROOMING: ★   PERSONALITY: ★★★

Labrador Retriever

Life's good; just ask a labrador. If these dogs have such a thing as a bad day, then they don't show it. Everything is fun in the labrador world and everything must be sniffed, licked and, if not bolted down, eaten. I can only imagine the place where these guys came from originally — it would have been a world of empty pantries, cleanly-licked dinner bowls and cleanly-licked owners. They are one of the few dogs that can actually work to earn their keep. As guide dogs, assistance dogs and sniffer dogs, their great qualities as gentle, loving creatures and highly food-motivated vacuum cleaners are used to full effect.

I know I shouldn't give them such a tough time about 'inhaling' their food (and things that could be confused as food), however, so many important points are based around this (big) part of their life. They are certainly prone to obesity and often, despite lots of exercise, their waistline continues to expand. So you have to be incredibly strict with their diet and feed only what they need and not what they claim they need. Make it a concentrated dry food to cut down on food bills as well as the waste produced. Carrying any extra pounds makes them at a high risk of arthritis, which is a degeneration of the joints. Having your pup, and especially its parents, checked out for signs of hip dysplasia and elbow problems is almost compulsory. Bad hips will mean a decreased quality of life and eventually a shortened life span. They certainly need lots of exercise, but make it the right type. Leash walks and runs are great, but swimming is even better. Try not to make them chase tennis balls or Frisbees for long periods. This stop-start, twisting-turning movement damages their delicate joints, making arthritis an early and unwelcome visitor. But rest assured they will love a chance to have a run or walk, no matter how long or short it might be. After all, there might be a bowl of food waiting at the end!

CHEAT NOTES

- Will make a great member of the family, but are time consuming.
- Give plenty of the right type of exercise.
- If not given enough attention and exercise, behavioural issues such as digging and barking are common.
- Feed only what is required. Don't give too many treats.
- Will shed a large amount of hair.
- Available in yellow, black, chocolate and even caramel colours. Note the appropriate use of food names!

TIME: ★★★★   SPACE: ★★★★   COST: ★★★★   EXERCISE: ★★★★   KIDS: ★★★★★
NOISE: ★★★   LIFESPAN: 11-13 years   GROOMING: ★★   PERSONALITY: ★★★★

Golden Retriever

If you have been, or are ever likely to be, paranoid about your own hairloss, my advice is to buy a golden retriever. The sheer volume of golden hair that is shed will put your issues into perspective. Just so long as you're not a blonde — otherwise it's going to be hard to tell whose hair is whose. They do shed large amounts, but of course, new hair is coming through all the time. You will find it like a trail of evidence, throughout the house, on your clothes and if you have a pool, clogging up the filter as well.

They are justifiably one of the most popular choices as a pet for kids and the family. They are gentle and understanding around children, but still playful and affectionate enough to have a huge amount of fun with grown-ups. Goldies make excellent guard dogs that pull off the good-cop / bad-cop routine beautifully, being great around the family but seemingly tough enough to keep intruders away.

Being a retriever, they love to swim. Which considering their build is a highly suitable exercise to be encouraged. Chances are that you will need to run or walk them as well, just to go close to tiring them out. Like the labrador, they live and love to eat, so exercise and careful control of their diet is essential to keeping them trim. With their large size, hip dysplasia and other structural problems (like elbow dysplasia) can have a big effect, so ensure you check both the puppy as well as its parents for any evidence of these problems. Skin allergies can also occur in the breed. All minor issues aside, they are one of the all-time great dogs for people of all ages and one that deserves its spot high-up on the list of most popular dog breeds. It won't take long for these dogs to win you over with their fun-loving personality.

CHEAT NOTES

- This breed is easy to track down — but be fussy about which pup you choose. Have a full vet check performed looking at the hips in particular.

- Make a great choice of pet for kids.

- Vary in colour from a light yellow right through to a dark gold. They tend to get darker and richer in colour with age. To predict what colour gold a golden retriever pup will end up, look at the colour of the ears — this will be close to the eventual colour of the whole dog.

- A daily brush will help to remove dead or loose hair before it ends up on you and your furniture.

TIME: ★★★★ SPACE: ★★★★ COST: ★★★★ EXERCISE: ★★★★ KIDS: ★★★★★
NOISE: ★★★ LIFESPAN: 11–13 years GROOMING: ★★★ PERSONALITY: ★★★★

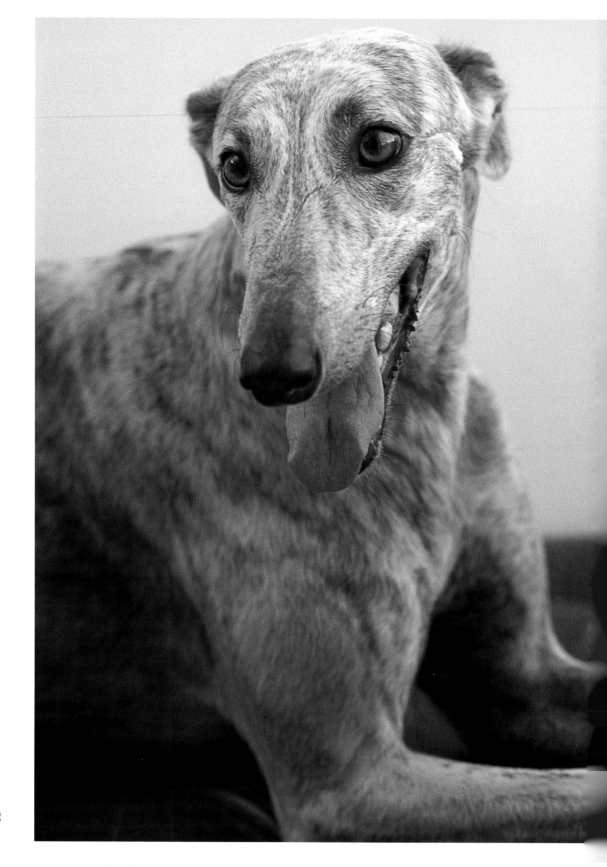

Greyhound

If you want a tip, the safest bet in greyhounds is having one as a pet. I have seen a lot of animals in my life, but this hound would have to be one of nature's most beautiful and gentle creatures. It seems the only place that life moves fast is on the racetrack — everything else is in slow motion. The comparisons are not unfair between them and a retired human athelete who sits on the back porch and takes floating journeys back to the time when the track roared like a landslide under their feet. They seem content with their life achievements to the point that life is now for lazing; those early mornings of the past must be repaid with late morning sleep-ins and afternoon siestas. You will soon see why adopting a greyhound and providing it with a life after racing is a truly odds-on good move.

Greyhounds are not high-maintenance dogs. Despite what their past and their build might tell you, exercise needn't be a big drain on their time or yours. A walk on the leash or a brief jog is enough. Remember, they are sprinters not marathon runners, so you don't have to be pounding the pavement to stop them knocking down walls. Now to the muzzle issue. The law in Australia says that they must be muzzled while they are outside their own yard. This is an outdated and flawed piece of legislature. They are no more of a threat to someone than say a maltese, and probably even less so. So don't let the muzzle put you off having one. Something you will need to do though, is always keep them on the lead. They are sight-hounds and love to run — and unless you're an olympic sprinter, if they start running you are unlikely to catch them.

Medically speaking they are a vet's nightmare. That is, vets would go out of business if everyone had greyhounds. They are true athletes, and as such, every cog in that machine is oiled and in full working order. They are not prone to any diseases. Even for a large dog, hip dysplasia isn't a danger.

CHEAT NOTES

- *Treat them gently as they can be rather sensitive.*
- *Often a coat is required in winter to keep them warm, after all, there's not much fat or fur to blanket them.*
- *This breed is probably the healthiest genetically.*
- *Looks can be deceiving — despite the muzzle, the greyhound is truly a gentle and beautiful animal.*
- *Minimal grooming is required as that short, sharp coat looks after itself.*
- *Greyhound adoption programs now operate across Australia.*

TIME: ★★ SPACE: ★★★ COST: ★★★ EXERCISE: ★★ KIDS: ★★★
NOISE: ★★ LIFESPAN: 11–14 years GROOMING: ★ PERSONALITY: ★★★

Rhodesian Ridgeback

When standing tall and proud, stripe of honour emblazoned down its back, the last thing you would expect is a transformation to the quivering, dribbling and uncertain shadow of a dog that often materialises not long after the tough facade has been dropped. To me, it's part of their charm and attraction that they can be menacing by appearance, but menaced in their every reaction. I even have a few clients that BYO towels for their dog's annual visit, such is the nervous dribble of urine that frequently signals the loss of composure.

This is a breed that will eat a lot, so keeping them in a healthy weight range can be a balancing act, especially when the 'I'm still hungry' routine is tried on you. Exercise is important for them, and you will need to set aside time at least once a day (preferably twice) to walk or run them.

How you train and treat a ridgeback will really make or break your time with them. They are intelligent and respond well to training so there should be no need to scold or shout at them. If you do, you are at great risk of either breaking their spirit and making them an insecure mess or at the other extreme, turning them into an aggressive animal, which isn't usually their game.

Being a big dog, there should be no surprises that the hips are a problem area. So, letting your dog become overweight is a big risk. Arthritis is likely to come into play in their later years. But being smart with the type of exercise you provide (keep it low-impact) and their weight, will help keep arthritis to a minimum. A tendency towards sensitive skin means the odd skin irritation, lump or bump, is seen in later life. Most of these aren't serious, however, all should be checked out as some may require surgery.

CHEAT NOTES

- Make an excellent family dog that is extremely loyal and patient around children.

- Only shampoo their coat if there is a need (bad odour, infection, overly dirty). They are prone to developing dry skin which is worsened by overbathing.

- The 'ridge' on the back is actually derived from a minor genetic anomaly. It causes no problems but has been deliberately bred in the dogs for its unique appearance.

- Do not be too firm with your training. A calm approach (and some patience) will achieve the best results.

- Remember, a big dog can mean big food bills.

TIME: ★★★★ SPACE: ★★★★ COST: ★★★★ EXERCISE: ★★★★ KIDS: ★★★
NOISE: ★★★ LIFESPAN: 11-13 years GROOMING: ★ PERSONALITY: ★★★

Bichon Frise

Yeah, alright you blokes out there. This certainly is a white fluffy dog. And as such, it might look a little strange in the back of the ute on the way to work, or as your running mate on a hard morning jog. Women might think it's cute, but around your mates the response might be a little stronger. This is a dog tailor-made for the good life — that white coat wouldn't look good covered in red dirt, so make your bichon's home an apartment or house. Otherwise, you will spend your whole life trying to keep them close to something resembling white.

The bichon believes in enjoying life and not getting too caught up in the territorial or dominance disputes that some other small, white fluff-balls may be prone to. They make happy (I swear they almost smile), friendly and independent pets that will endear themselves to their owners. Being into life as they are, the bichon tends to take care of most of its own exercise requirements. However, a walk and a run at the park are met with big enthusiasm.

In comparison to breeds of a similar size, they are pretty hardy. Still, watch out for dislocating kneecaps (due to a poorly aligned knee joint). They may not be obvious in a pup, but any hopping or limping on the back legs of the parents should be treated with suspicion. A vet should be able to assess whether the knee joints of pups are likely to develop problems. Eye problems are the other area of worry. Blocked tear ducts are common and result in the dirty staining around the inner corner of the eyes. Ongoing cleaning is usually required. Cataracts are also an issue, so look to the parents for any evidence that they have developed the eye problem and try to avoid these bloodlines.

CHEAT NOTES

- *A small dog that doesn't have small dog syndrome — and that's a good thing.*

- *Although relatively medically sound, they do require regular grooming to keep them clean and knot free. Remember that this can be costly and time consuming.*

- *Check the parents for evidence of dislocating kneecaps. This can be a painful and costly annoyance in later life.*

- *A great first family pet.*

TIME: ★★★ SPACE: ★★ COST: ★★★★ EXERCISE: ★★ KIDS: ★★★★
NOISE: ★★ LIFESPAN: 11–13 years GROOMING: ★★★★★ PERSONALITY: ★★★

Labradoodle

If you think the name sounds strange — it could have been so much worse. Just be thankful that on that balmy summer night when the labrador and poodle decided to get friendly, the bulldog and the shih tzu were not thinking along the same lines. Today, crossbreeding seems to be as much about getting the best out of both breeds' names, as it does about making the most out of their genes. But thankfully, the labradoodle is here to stay, and along with it, the shaggy-dog look, which I reckon is so underrated. Any old dog can pull off the 'just cut' look with its neat, regular edges, but it takes serious Afro-style to master the shag.

The breed's strength lies in one of the main benefits of crossbreeding — obtaining 'hybrid vigour'. This is essentially getting the best of both breeds. In the case of the labradoodle, it is the fun-loving personality and temperament of the labrador, with the intelligence of the poodle. This combination makes for what is always a unique situation — a dog that not only loves a good time, but actually knows how and when to get it. For this reason, most families that have them describe them as being scarily human-like, and a major part of the family. It should seem obvious then that they require a reasonable amount of human contact to allow them to vent some of this enthusiasm. Most labradoodles won't shed hair as they carry on the genes of the wool-like poodle coat — making them an advantageous breed for asthma and allergy sufferers, but not a guaranteed allergy-free animal.

Medically speaking, the cross does go close to eliminating the hereditary problems of the two contributing breeds, while not creating new ones. It's important to remember though, that crossbreeding isn't an instant recipe for success — if the problem is in both parents, then it's almost a certainty for the offspring, whether a crossbreed or not. Hip dysplasia is always an issue in medium and large breeds, however, the use of the miniature poodle (as a father, thankfully) has helped to minimise this. Skin allergies and infections are probably the most common problem seen by a vet. Although, never forget the value of a full check-up and examination of the parents. A check of the eyes for PRA (progressive retinal atrophy) is advisable.

CHEAT NOTES

- Doesn't shed a lot of hair, making it a good choice for allergy sufferers.
- They come in straight- and curly-haired varieties.
- Personality-plus dogs. Great for young families or active people that want a mate and a dog.
- Don't get your pup too 'revved up'. The combination of intelligence and energy needs to be controlled and, of course, enjoyed.

TIME: ★★★★ SPACE: ★★★ COST: ★★★ EXERCISE: ★★★★ KIDS: ★★★★
NOISE: ★★ LIFESPAN: 12–14 years GROOMING: ★★★ PERSONALITY: ★★★★★

Boxer

Those people out there that are lucky enough to own a boxer often have more in common than just a love of big dogs with big jowls. There is a distinct interior decorating pattern — highlighted by strings of saliva on the walls. There are always a number of rolls of kitchen paper in the cupboard, for correcting the aforementioned interior design. And there are a lack of vases, ornaments and heirlooms on low-lying tables and benchtops, absent for fear of a breakage due to the vibrant energy and excitement that so frequently bubbles over from this entertaining and extraverted dog.

This dog is a major people pleaser. Its every action and thought is seemingly centred around enjoyment of some kind. They are no shrinking violet. They love attention and exercise and the more extravagant, the better. Although, they could become bored if playtime is not forthcoming. They make great family pets, but a word of warning — small children may find their leaping around a little intimidating. They do, however, bond closely to all family members. The measure of how strong and lovable their personality can be is shown by the way, like probably no other breed I have seen, anyone that has had or known a boxer will always make an effort to talk to or play with a boxer and its owner. This is quite unique.

Unfortunately, living their life to the full acts as a sort of compensation for these dogs. They don't generally live long lives. Heart conditions (called aortic stenosis, or boxer cardiomyopathy), inflammatory bowel diseases (boxer colitis), hip problems and a tendency to develop skin tumours and occasionally, brain tumours, can shorten their lifespan. Where possible, have these issues checked out by the breeder and by your vet to see if they are present, or likely to be present, in your boxer.

CHEAT NOTES

- *An energetic and entertaining pet. Will require a lot of exercise.*
- *Minimal grooming, but keeping the house clean around them can be an effort.*
- *Prone to a number of diseases so get friendly with your local vet.*
- *A check of the family history is essential.*

TIME: ★★★★ SPACE: ★★★★ COST: ★★★★ EXERCISE: ★★★★ KIDS: ★★★★
NOISE: ★★ LIFESPAN: 9–12 years GROOMING: ★ PERSONALITY: ★★★★★

Poodle

The poodle never meant to, but it almost can't help but polarise people. You either absolutely adore them or, at the other end of the scale, could never imagine sharing a couch with one. The funny thing is that given half a chance to work their way into your lives, it won't be too long before you too are a poodle person.

Like no other breed, the poodle comes in an amazing variety of sizes and colours — from the tiny toy up to a massive standard, and in flavours like apricot, silver and black. But though their dimensions may vary, a few traits remain common to all. This is an intelligent breed, they are easily trained, but should always be treated like a dog, not a person, for fear of them becoming a little neurotic. If you've seen a precious poodle you'll know why I say this — for a small dog they can have a lot of attitude. The poodle won't shed hair as its coat is more like a fleece. But it will require a daily brush or comb through. The coat grows continuously so will need a regular shearing at your local grooming salon. How you clip them is obviously up to you. For those that aren't too sure about the walking pom-pom look, then an all-over clip that slowly matures into an Afro can be a bit of a hit. Finally, we come to the 'prance'. That graceful glide that makes you convinced those feet don't even touch the ground. Whether a toy or a standard, this mode of transport is a given.

If you don't want your poodle on a first name basis with your vet, then here's what you need to check. Start with the eyes: the breed is prone to PRA (progressive retinal atrophy, a degenerative eye condition) and cataracts (in later life), so check that some testing has been performed on your pup and its parents. And even though their type of coat gains a lot of attention, any hair that makes its way into the ears just isn't welcome. It will trap moisture and make your dog prone to smelly and sore ear infections, so have this plucked regularly. Mobility isn't a renowned problem, especially in comparison to other small breeds, although ensure a check for slipping kneecaps is made. Finally, if you are looking to up-size your poodle to a standard, check out the hips for hip dysplasia and the heart (congenital heart defects are seen).

CHEAT NOTES

- There are three sizes: toy (3–5 kg/6½–11 lb); miniature (5–8 kg/11–17½ lb); and standard (20–35 kg/44–77 lb).

- The standard poodle has one of the more 'special' personalities in the dog world. It's scarily human-like and very intelligent.

- The coat is renowned as being low-allergy as it won't shed.

TIME: ★★★   SPACE: ★★ (standard ★★★★)   COST: ★★★ (increases with size)
.EXERCISE: ★★ (standard ★★★)   KIDS: ★★★   NOISE: ★★★   LIFESPAN: 12-14 years
(standard 9-13 years)   GROOMING: ★★★★   PERSONALITY: ★★★ (standard ★★★★★)

Staffordshire Bull Terrier

It seems like every day is a great day if you are a staffie. Unlike pets that prefer the easy life of eating and sleeping, this 'keg on legs' is all hustle and bustle. And it's probably the 110 per cent life philosophy that makes them so popular with pet owners. It's rare that you'll be left in any doubt as to a staffie's opinion on any matter — such is their capacity to act out and often vocalise their feelings.

It surprises many people that this dog can be such a sook. They are incredibly sensitive and have a real need to feel loved and part of the family unit. Yet a lot of people still see a staffie as an aggressive dog. It's very unlike a staffie to be aggressive to a person; although you should never trust any dog you are unfamiliar with. Most problems occur when a staffie has been trained to be aggressive or a staffie is actually confused for a pit bull in the first place. The only real risk with the breed is probably around other dogs. They can become overly protective of their owners and themselves, so it's important that you socialise your pup extensively by making it meet and greet all sorts of other pets and people.

This is a highly exuberant and playful breed that is great with kids, but just bear in mind that small kids under the age of five may be easily 'bowled over' in the rush for your dog to be a part of something fun. Nevertheless, how much a staffie bonds to its family is a big plus, provided that bond doesn't go too far. Separation anxiety is quite common and should be managed early before excess barking, digging or even staffie-singing results.

This is obviously not an Australian breed, so acclimatising to our weather can be difficult. Being dark in colour and having a relatively compressed nose and face (and an overly long soft palate), means they are prone to heat stress if exercised in the hottest part of the day. Always ensure there is plenty of cool drinking water. Their skin is also sensitive to allergens, so the odd skin infection and irritation is common. Skin allergies are commonly passed from generation to generation, so ensure the parents are itch-free. Finally, breeding staffies can carry risks. Many pregnant bitches require a caesarean when the pup's head is unable to pass through the narrow pelvis.

CHEAT NOTES

- *A very content 'inside' dog.*
- *Makes a great family pet and is good with kids, provided they aren't too small.*
- *Don't require a huge amount of exercise, but be sure to avoid excess weight and obesity.*
- *The major medical problems revolve around skin allergies and heat stress.*

TIME: ★★★★ SPACE: ★★★ COST: ★★★ EXERCISE: ★★★ KIDS: ★★★
NOISE: ★★★ LIFESPAN: 12-13 years GROOMING: ★ PERSONALITY: ★★★★★

Spoodle

Despite looking more like a dancing floor rug than one of the up-and-coming dog breeds, the spoodle (a cross between a cocker spaniel and a poodle) will not only be a faithful friend but is also guaranteed to be a true entertainer. They have a keen sense of fun and seem to be always in search of new and exciting energy-expending activities. For a young family, they would make a worthy adversary for a seven year old kid intent on playing from sunup to sundown. While this playful side is one of their true attractions, in the wrong situation it could also be one of their downfalls. This isn't a low maintenance dog that you can feed and forget. They do expect attention and exercise, and if they don't get it then they can be a little destructive, chewing their way through shoes and furniture. But a little exercise in the morning and at night along with some activities to occupy them during the day should do the trick. While this breed can be a little active, they are not as needy, nor on the same level of attention deficit as the small terriers or the maltese, and would make a reasonable apartment pet — provided there was some exercise provided.

It's important to remember that this is still a recently established crossbreed. However, the theory behind crossbreeding says that issues present in both the parents will probably be found in the pups. With this in mind, keeping the long, floppy and fluffy ears free of infection is going to be difficult. Moisture and excess wax should be removed whenever possible, along with any unwanted and entirely decorative 'ear hair'. Be sure to keep the hair away from the eyes as well. Any rubbing on the eyeball will cause soreness and even conjunctivitis. Have the eyes checked for any genetic diseases (like PRA) that have been reported in the spoodle. The leg joints (especially the hips, elbows and knees) should get a thorough once-over to detect any structural problems.

CHEAT NOTES

- Because of the poodle genes, the spoodle should not shed hair. It means that you won't get the hair on you, but regular brushing will be required.

- Put the time in with the breed and they will be a great pet. Training is essential.

- Ensure they don't become too dependent on you. Separation anxiety can result if they become too obsessed with people.

- An entertaining dog to have around. Kids will love their endless energy and bubbly personality.

TIME: ★★★★ SPACE: ★★★ COST: ★★★ EXERCISE: ★★★ KIDS: ★★★★
NOISE: ★★★ LIFESPAN: 12–13 years GROOMING: ★★★★ PERSONALITY: ★★★★

176

CATS

It's not hard to see why people become intrigued and sometimes even confused by cats. Their daily existence is complex in some respects, yet simple in others. For on one hand, the busy feline is flat-out maintaining that ice-cool demeanour, clean-cut appearance and dominance over their little slice of territory, while on the other, their insistence on the 20 hours of sleep per day suggests a different beast altogether. Whatever conclusion you draw on the feline, there is one word that sums up the little guy — cool. While a dog dishes out affection to anyone and anything within patting range, the cat is entirely different. It makes you earn it. And you can't help but respect that.

And while the cats' arch enemy boasts greater variation in size, the cat well and truly makes up for it with the diversity in colour, coat types and personalities across the breeds. There are blues, whites, browns, greys, blacks, oranges, reds as well as tabby and tortoiseshell colours and patterns adorning coats that might be long, medium, short, or not even there at all. Cats can be timid and shy, or gregarious and playful. But despite all this variation, the one constant is that cool demeanour that never leaves them.

It's been said that there are cat people and there are non-cat people. I disagree. Instead, I believe 'non-cat' people haven't spent quite enough time around cats. The beauty of a cat is that it doesn't give you all it's got at first glance. It reveals a little bit of itself every now and then, but keeps you on a need-to-know basis until you're ready for more. Cats can be intricate to the extreme, but are always fascinating. The confusion is there for a reason — it keeps you interested and coming back for more.

Moggie (Domestic Shorthair Cat)

The moggie is your ultimate survivor breed of cat. Not bred to look or act a certain way but simply bred to be a cat; which they do so well. The parents of moggies typically didn't read the romantic love stories; in their prime they were probably more of a believer in the 'boy meets girl, boy never sees girl again and girl gets kittens 9 weeks later' sort of love story. If you could look at a moggie's family tree it would look more like one of those giant 400 year old trees in a National Park, rather than the ordered and manicured pedigree that you see with pure-bred cats. But the reality is that this is probably the best thing for them. They are as tough as an old pair of boots. With such a variety of genes, they tend to have the best of all their relatives combined into one neat package. And what a hardy, yet diverse package it can be. There's more colours in the range for your moggie than there are on show at a 1980s themed dress-up party.

Where you choose your moggie from is up to you. Breeders typically won't 'breed' them because they aren't seen as 'pure' enough. So it's really down to the pet stores or pounds to pick out your cat. If you are choosing from one of these sources, it's hard to know if the kittens or cats have been strays before they have come to be sold. The real significance of this is in the fact that stray cats, through their existence on the streets, are exposed to many different cats as well as their viruses and infections. Many of these viruses, like FIV (feline aids),

FeLV (feline leukaemia) and cat flu, can have serious implications, so bear this in mind. Remember, if your pet inspection turns up any sniffles or other signs of sickness, then steer clear of that cat. Behaviourally speaking, ex-stray kittens should be fine provided they are taken off the streets early enough. It makes sense, however, to watch the kitten for any signs of feral behaviour.

On the whole, if you can get a good one, your moggie should be a tough little furball that will last for years. Being a crossbreed, their traits and requirements tend to be a combination of all the other breeds put together. And with their history of 'doing their own thing', they tend to be low-maintenance and not at all needy.

CHEAT NOTES

- *Make sure you buy a disease-free moggie and it will be around for many years.*

- *Desex it at 6 months of age.*

- *Just because it doesn't have pedigree papers doesn't mean it won't be healthy — it's often just the opposite. These are hardy and healthy cats.*

TIME: ★★ **SPACE:** ★ **COST:** ★★ **EXERCISE:** ★ **KIDS:** ★★★ **NOISE:** ★
LIFESPAN: 12–17 years **GROOMING:** ★★ **PERSONALITY:** variable from ★★ to ★★★

Burmilla

I'm currently involved in an ongoing battle with a burmilla. And I'm not sure if it tells more about their personality as a breed, or uncovers some insecurities of my own. This burmilla was found as a stray out in the country, sneaking his way between the dry, brown clumps of tussock grass. As a stray, he had no great prospects apart from a life of crime and infidelity. So he was taken by his new owners and bought into the city to my clinic where I first laid eyes on him. If he wasn't already put-out by the experience of moving to the city, he was when I informed his owners that he wasn't the tough, 'rough around the edges' country kid he was claiming, but was instead a pure-bred burmilla, probably raised by a designer mother on a luxury farmlet. As I was holding the newly outed fraudster, he returned fire upon his accuser, unleashing a torrent of a pungent, golden liquid all over my work trousers. He was my first customer of the day — it would be a rather aromatic clinic for the remainder. As a way of exacting my revenge, he found himself castrated not 2 hours later. Chris 2, Cat 1. I know he is waiting to even the score. Vaccination time approaches and I am a little concerned.

The interesting thing was that even though this country kid had fallen in with the wrong crowd, he quickly corrected his ways and became a true-to-form burmilla. It's a cat that's like a food hall in a shopping centre — it's got a bit of everything. They are relaxed cats as adults yet occasionally (for your entertainment) will tear around the house in a electric burst of energy. They are playful and affectionate, but at the same time not demanding or aloof. If they were any more balanced and well-rounded they would be a ball. They also make good-looking cats. They come is a spectrum of colours including black, lilac, chocolate and red. They also have large luminous green or amber eyes, which they tend to flash.

The great thing about the breed is that there are no significant medical concerns. They don't seem to be genetically predisposed to anything of note. With such a good, healthy starting point it's important to do the basics well. Desexing around 6 months, regular worming and vaccinations, and ensuring they are fed a high-quality diet of dry food and the odd raw chicken wing should see them sail into their teenage years with any luck.

CHEAT NOTES

- Perfect for apartments.

- Some, but not a large amount of grooming is required. Brush well at least once a week.

- Originally a cross between a Burmese and a Chinchilla.

- A curious and affectionate breed, but not too demanding — a perfect mix.

TIME: ★★ SPACE: ★★ COST: ★★ EXERCISE: ★ KIDS: ★★★★
NOISE: ★ LIFESPAN: 13–15 years GROOMING: ★★ PERSONALITY: ★★★

Burmese

Burmese cats always remind me of that cheeky kid in school that could never sit still and always wanted to be the involved in all the action. Even though half the time you knew they were doing the wrong thing and you shouldn't, you couldn't help but like them. Burmese make the funniest kittens — they are everything a hyperactive 4 year old child, after eating a bucket of mixed lollies (candy), could ever hope to be and more. Even though they do mellow slightly with age, this love of adventure and the taste for chaos never really leaves them. One of the most amusing features of them is that if they are having fun by themselves, then they won't be shy to take the fun to you. They truly crave attention and will do anything to get it.

The way the breed has developed, they have become the true indoor specialist. As much as this little character would love to unleash himself upon the outside world, he just isn't cut out for it. So, like other items of indoor furniture, leaving your burmese outside to see how it goes will only end in trouble. Being almost 100 per cent indoors has important implications though. You will have to limit their food intake to ensure they don't become obese (a common burmese curse), and ensure you have a good scratching post and toys to burn off the seemingly unending energy supply. They are generally a healthy cat, however, it's obviously best to prevent problems before they occur. It's important that you pick a kitten that is free of cat flu and other signs of sickness (see the pet inspection section). Importantly, try to prevent the all too common occurrence of them getting themselves into trouble. Avoiding busy roads, high balconies and other cats will certainly cut down on your vet bills.

CHEAT NOTES

- A very 'in your face' cat, but a laugh a minute.

- Low grooming requirement. A good brush once a week is enough.

- Should be kept indoors all the time, or only have supervised excursions outside.

- Keep nails trimmed short to stop you bearing the scars of their youthful exuberance.

TIME: ★★★   SPACE: ★★   COST: ★★★   EXERCISE: ★★   KIDS: ★★★
NOISE: ★★★   LIFESPAN: 10-13 years   GROOMING: ★   PERSONALITY: ★★★★

Australian Mist (Spotted Mist)

So, should you be patriotic and support the 'home-grown' product? Every expert agrees that the aussie mist is an affectionate and playful cat. It's also accepted that they can have their laid back moments. But this to me has always been an understatement. I am convinced that one day this Australian will master the art of kicking the footy in the park with some mates before settling back in the sun with a tinny on a banana lounge beside the pool. And you think I'm joking? I actually know of an aussie mist that is so obsessed with human company and finding a warm lap to lie in, that it had to go on medication to ease the urge — and allow its owners some space and time to themselves.

They are about as human-like as a cat gets, and their owners (and their vets) are often bemused by them for that reason. They will supervise the households comings and goings, and are understanding yet fun-loving around children. Their attitude to life doesn't sit well in the rough and tumble of the outside world, so they are often better off kept inside for their own safety.

They have been well-bred and so are relatively free of inherited diseases. The only point worthy of a mention is skin allergies — some bloodlines are prone to them, so check out the parents of the kitten you are after for any signs. Licking, scratching and saliva staining (a brown discolouration on the fur) around the feet, groin, thighs and lower back can be clues to the problem. And yes, that means that in the case of these affected Australian mist cats, they are actually allergic to Australia.

Some people can confuse the aussie mist for a tabby moggie, however, look for the trademark spots and tiger-like stripes on the legs and flanks. The spots may be brown, blue, chocolate, lilac, gold or peach in colour, but always lie over a creamy background.

CHEAT NOTES

- *A true Australian. Laid back and loves good company. A perfect pet for kids and family.*
- *The short, dense coat isn't high-maintenance, but will need regular grooming to remove excess hair and avoid furballs.*
- *Generally free of genetic disease.*
- *Not suited to life outside the confines of a house or apartment.*

TIME: ★★ SPACE: ★★ COST: ★★ EXERCISE: ★ KIDS: ★★★★★
NOISE: ★ LIFESPAN: 12-15 years GROOMING: ★★ PERSONALITY: ★★★★

British Shorthair

I think someone needs to tell these Brits that the weather in Australia isn't quite the same as it is back home. It's the only reason I can find why this pom insists on living the good life on the couch in the comfort of the home. And you won't hear a complaint or anything near a whinge about that from them. As an owner, you shouldn't be complaining either, as it makes for one of the most companionable and easy-going cats in the world. For someone working long hours that wants a friendly face to come home to, this Brit may make the perfect companion.

Their chubby cheeks makes them look much like a teddy bear and they can make a fairly good impression of one with their behaviour. The only downside is that they can sometimes be too reserved, and may require a game to lure them out of their retirement mode. They are reasonably sound medically, although a routine check is mandatory. Because of their chubby cheeks and flat nose, a case of cat flu in this breed can severely compromise their breathing capacity. So ensure there are no signs of any snuffles in your kitten. Check with the breeders for proof that the kidneys of your kitten and its parents have been certified as free of any problems. Kidney diseases used to be an issue in the breed, however, intelligent breeding and thorough checks of bloodlines have reduced its occurrence dramatically.

The lack of physical activity can make obesity a common consequence of the life of leisure. To counter this, feed a light (low-calorie) diet and use energy-burning games, such as chasing ping-pong balls, laser pointers and feather lures, to work off that weight.

CHEAT NOTES

- A scarily relaxed cat.
- A good brush once or twice a week takes care of the grooming.
- One for the kids. Amazingly tolerant of ankle-biters. Suited to hard-working people.
- Most popular colours are blue, tortoiseshell and black. Tabby patterns are available in all colours.
- Watch their waistline — they are prone to obesity, which can cause arthritis, diabetes and kidney problems.

TIME: ★★ SPACE: ★ COST: ★★ EXERCISE: ★ KIDS: ★★★★★
NOISE: ★ LIFESPAN: 10–13 years GROOMING: ★★ PERSONALITY: ★★★

Birman

If you believe the stories regarding the emergence of this breed, you will understand why the Birman now likes to sleep a lot. They have certainly been busy. Apparently once the sacred temple cats of Burma, their white feet were meant to have been spiritually gifted to them. Fast forward to the present day and they are well and truly making their presence felt in Australia as an up-and-comer in cat circles. It probably revolves around their possession of a Persian-like coat, their deep blue eyes, and a playful yet settled temperament.

These cats mark themselves as something special right from the start. Their months as a kitten are amusing to say the least. They are cheeky little beasts, but like a cocky supermodel, seem to be aware of their good looks and know only too well what they can and can't get away with. Their meow can be loud and distinctive, so ensuring that you don't give into their every whim might make them a little less demanding, and make any vocal disapproval of their situation less likely.

Those people that tend to have a trouble-free Birman are those that do the basics right. Feed a well-balanced diet (a premium brand dry food is ideal) and ensure some raw chicken wings are available to keep those teeth clean. As with any pure-bred cat, have their kidneys checked out prior to purchase. Focus most of your attention of that thick silky coat. You must brush them regularly (twice a day is often required) to avoid the loose hair causing furballs. Excess hair that is digested can also combine with an interesting trait of a narrow pelvis, to make constipation a big risk. In my opinion, this is probably the most serious issue with the breed.

CHEAT NOTES

- A stunning breed with an equally stunning past.

- Do the basics right.

- Any problems often start and end with that thick silky coat. Brush it regularly and the hair will end up in the brush and not in their gut or on you.

- Grooming may be time consuming.

- For someone after a long-haired cat, this makes a smart choice.

- Ask about any history of constipation in the parents.

TIME: ★★★ SPACE: ★ COST: ★★★ EXERCISE: ★ KIDS: ★★★
NOISE: ★★ LIFESPAN: 10–13 years GROOMING: ★★★★★ PERSONALITY: ★★★

Russian Blue

It's probably a good sign that owners of russian blues seem to spend more time thinking up a suitable name for their cats (like Boris, Igor or Vladimir) than they do spending time and money at their local vet clinic. Their exact place of origin is unknown, but was thought, unsurprisingly, to be somewhere in Russia. Today, they are a popular breed worldwide, largely due to their good health and adaptable, easy-to-please personality.

There are few situations where the russian blue won't feel at home. Apartments don't faze them and they'll quite happily live indoors or out. Even other pets are accepted, or maybe tolerated in the case of some I'm sure. They like some play time which the kids will enjoy, however, they do reach their limit of tolerance when there is too much noise or movement, resulting in them becoming a little withdrawn. In a family situation they are known to pick a favourite to which they will be most strongly bonded.

There are no major health concerns so provided you take care of the basics — vaccinations, worming, flea control and keep the weight down and the teeth clean — this is one cat that can live for a long time. The only point worth mentioning is something quite bizarre. It sounds strange, but I've seen a few russian blues (and it's also been reported elsewhere) that have exhibited some pretty odd behaviours such as 'suckling' on their owners clothing or fingers, as if suckling its mother, and also chewing particular items (rugs, carpets, chairs, shoes) around the house that become favourites. This is certainly a rare occurance and mentioned only for your interest.

CHEAT NOTES

- *A playful, yet placid pet.*
- *Adaptable to whatever house conditions you provide, as long as its not too wild in there.*
- *Minimal grooming required. A brush a couple of times a week is ideal.*
- *No major health problems reported.*

TIME: ★★ SPACE: ★★ COST: ★★ EXERCISE: ★ KIDS: ★★★
NOISE: ★ LIFESPAN: 13-17 years GROOMING: ★ PERSONALITY: ★★★

Ragdoll

How the ragdoll earned its name says a lot about the suitability of this cat as a family pet. Whether it shows a strong survival instinct or just plain tolerance I'm not too sure; but the ragdoll's tendency to go limp when handled does make it a cat to consider for kids that can be a little rough.

It's not just the kids that will find this laid back persona appealing. Big kids, living in apartments, find them to be a cat that becomes a much loved and much laughed at little guy. As what people soon realise is that this ice-cool character isn't what you get all day everyday. Moments of mayhem will certainly keep things interesting, as when it's playtime — it's certainly playtime.

They have some size to throw around too. Most ragdolls will weigh around 8 kg (18 lb) making them a heavyweight in the cat world. This means food bills will be slightly higher and there will be a lot more cat to brush than you might think. Breeders maintain that the semi-longhaired coat is resistant to matting, however, like any cat with some length in the locks, regular daily brushing is the only true preventative step to stop knotting and large amounts of moulting over your favourite black top. You do, however, have four choices of hair colour for your cat (and your black top): chocolate, seal, lilac and blue. The large oval deep-blue eyes are another big feature of the breed. But be warned, your cat will use them for evil as well as good; you may find it hard to say no to them.

Proper screening of the parents is essential with any pure-bred cat. In the case of the ragdoll, a heart condition (called a cardiomyopathy) and a kidney problem (called polycystic kidney disease) are the two 'must-mention' items when talking to the breeder. Ensure there is no history of these in the parents of your kitten. Obviously, a healthy diet with a good mix of mostly dry food and some raw chicken wings, and regular top-ups of vaccinations and worming, as well as checkups at your vet are the key to a long happy life. Some ragdolls will live up to 15 years.

CHEAT NOTES

- A laid-back cat that knows that kids can be conquered just by keeping it cool.

- Perfect for apartment living.

- Brush the coat regularly to avoid knots and excess hair shedding.

- Check the family for evidence of cardiomyopathy and polycystic kidney disease.

TIME: ★★★   SPACE: ★   COST: ★★★   EXERCISE: ★   KIDS: ★★★★
NOISE: ★★   LIFESPAN: 12–15 years   GROOMING: ★★★★   PERSONALITY: ★★★

BIRDS

Talkative little birds have the potential to transform your home into a bird sanctuary. As a vet, however, I'm always reluctant about putting birds in cages. They are energetic animals with active minds and bodies. Make no mistake, some birds do not cope with a life behind bars — these tend to become frustrated by a lack of stimulation. Remember that in the wild, many birds fly around 50 km (30 miles) a day, constantly kept alert by having to hunt for food and stay away from predators. In a cage, life is simple — there are no threats and food is available in an all-you-can eat buffet. This may sound easy, but it's not natural for most birds, so I will only recommend those breeds that do handle the isolation and new way of life.

If you do decide to keep a bird, strap yourself in, they are incredibly funny and intelligent creatures that will keep you on your toes. They may seem healthy but things can change quickly when you're that small — so keep a close watch. Here's some ideas to reduce the risk, while improving the life of birds:

- Keep them at their right temperature. If a bird gets too cold (or hot) then it becomes stressed, making sickness almost a matter of time. Find out what your bird's natural environment is (desert, rainforest, and so on) and mimic the temperature. Use a heat-lamp positioned on the side of the cage, as well as a blanket over the top of the cage to increase the warmth.

- Keep them out of cold drafts. Many people hang cages up, or have them on high stands. This serves to isolate the bird and put it at the mercy of any cool winds that can rush through the cage. In the wild, birds will huddle together or find a warm spot to keep healthy.

- Watch out for signs of sickness. Birds are great actors and won't show any ill health until it's often too late. Classic warning signs of sickness are the fluffed-up look (where the feathers are ruffled all over), any decrease or increase in appetite, lack of activity, sitting on the floor of the cage, vomiting, diarrhoea, going quiet, or the tail-bob that moves the tail up and down.

- Give them something to do. Bored birds become frustrated and aren't happy or healthy animals. Place branches of native plants to provide some entertainment as they shred and chew the plant material. As a general (but not complete) rule, native plants are non-toxic to birds. Other measures to avoid boredom include providing some suitable toys, as birds love things to chew, play with and look at. You should also encourage birds to preen themselves — it's a good way to keep a bird busy and entertained. Spray a fine mist of water using an atomiser over the bird to encourage preening. But don't overdo it, as it can make birds cold. As a final measure to keep your bird entertained, put on the television or radio. Birds can and do watch television, and it stops their mind from getting bored.

- Don't overfeed your bird. Birds that don't fly large distances don't need large amounts of food. A high seed diet that contains a lot of oil is likely to make them fat. An average-sized budgie only requires 1 teaspoon of seed twice a day. Add some variety (and vitamins) to the food by adding in some fresh vegies. Do not feed lettuce, as this causes diarrhoea. The most important thing with feeding birds is to identify exactly what it is that they eat in the wild.

Canary

This is one bird that is truly content being kept in a cage, and their chirpy little song is a sign that life's good. But the interesting fact about canaries is that they won't all chirp. Its only the males that can sing and their performances are all in the name of one thing — love. This means that the moment you pair a male with a female, he'll stop. After all, he's found what he's looking for. In addition to this, it's only breeding season that brings on the love songs. So it's all Barry White and Tom Jones from spring until the end of summer before he packs the records, cologne and roses away for another year. In the end, it's up to you whether you like him single or not. As, at least for you, his bachelor lifestyle does have its upsides.

People imagine canaries as being yellow, when in fact they now come in an impressive rainbow of eye-catching colours. Selective breeding has allowed this change to occur, but you can play a part as well. It's possible to use feed supplements to enrich their colours. These are available from pet stores and contain pigments that, once eaten, can find their way into the feather colour of your bird.

As always, make a thorough check of your bird before you even think about taking it home. Canaries should always look bright and alert and be active to the point of being hyperactive. Any bird that sits by itself and doesn't seem interested in flying or looks fluffed-up should be avoided — these are sick birds. Look to ensure they not only fly well, but that their little feet are able to perch naturally. The most serious condition of canaries is air sac mites. These mites infect the lining of the little air-filled pockets that store and feed air into the lungs. Any bird with air sac mites finds it difficult to breathe and may wheeze and struggle for air. You can detect the disease two ways: either listen to the bird breathe yourself by putting your ear to their chest and listening for wheezing; or make the birds fly around their aviary — any bird that stops soon after and perches, while struggling to breathe, is possibly infected.

CHEAT NOTES

- Remember that it's the males that chirp. Either get another male or leave him by himself if you want him to keep on chirping.

- This is one bird that is truly content with being in a cage. But with cages, it's a case of the bigger the better.

- Like any bird, these guys can be a little fragile. Go easy on them and make sure kids know that they are not a toy.

- Never let your bird get too cold and don't overfeed him.

- A low-maintenance but energetic and interesting little pet.

TIME: ★ SPACE: ★ COST: ★ EXERCISE: ☆ KIDS: ★★
NOISE: ★ (males) LIFESPAN: 1–7 years GROOMING: ☆ PERSONALITY: ★★

Budgie

Not many people know that the budgie is about as true-blue Australian as it gets. After humble beginnings as a small bird in the deserts of central Australia, this little battler has become well-known internationally. The interesting thing is that they were originally a green colour, but now (after a bit of a dip in the genetic paint tin) they come in almost every colour around. The blues and greens tend to be the most popular. However, part of the fun is discovering all the colour combinations that are available.

The main attraction with budgies is that they can be a pet for all the family. They are a little tougher than canaries, so may be a better choice for kids, especially if you're looking for a bird that you can enjoy out of its cage. If you do take your budgie out of its cage, first ensure that you turn off any ceiling fans and shut any open windows.

When choosing a budgie, ensure that their feet and legs function normally. Make a special effort to inspect around the nostrils and the beak for any signs of a beak mite called scaly face mite, which can give the area a moth-eaten or honeycomb look. This is easily treated by a vet, but should be identified early before the signs become too dramatic.

Originally being an active desert bird, the budgie can get a little fed-up with being kept in a small cage. And 'fed up' is an appropriate term. They can suffer from boredom which can lead to strange behaviours, such as feather picking, where they actually pull their own feathers out.

The lack of exercise and the 'all you can eat' food and beverage service in their cage can make them look quite 'fed up' also. Obesity is a big issue if your budgie isn't exercised enough, or is fed too much. Fatty lumps, a weakened immune system and a shortened lifespan are all the result of a budgie's bulging belly. Be sure when you are formulating a diet for your budgie that you include plenty of green leafy vegetables (but not lettuce) and throw in some native plants which will keep them occupied.

CHEAT NOTES

- Budgies, although tougher than canaries, still need special care. Their small size means they are susceptible to getting sick quickly.

- Don't feed them too much.

- Some sort of exercise, such as flying around a secure room in the house, helps to keep the bird's weight down.

- Budgies tolerate, but don't love, cage living. The bigger the cage, the better.

- 1 teaspoon of seed twice a day (with some greens) is enough food for an average-sized budgie.

TIME: ★★ SPACE: ★ COST: ★ EXERCISE: ★ KIDS: ★★★
NOISE: ★ LIFESPAN: 3 months–10 years GROOMING: ☆ PERSONALITY: ★★★

Fish

Bringing the magic of the sea into your own lounge room will make it look amazing and provide a major talking point with any people lucky enough to visit your own personal indoor aquarium. And no matter whether we're talking large or small, there is always that sense of calm and relaxation that comes with being, or just seeing, underwater. But what you must realise is that fish aren't just fed and forgotten. You must choose the right type of fish for you; those that suit your aquarium and your life as well. Then, you must maintain and watch over their waterworld. Almost all of the problems associated with keeping fish come about from not being able to meet all the needs that those particular fish have. You must remember that their water is their home, as well as their toilet — so if you want to prevent them from going to the big flushing toilet in the sky, you must keep it clean and at the right temperature and pH level for their needs.

Consider for a moment how much time you have available to care for your fish and who will be looking after them. The more complex aquarium types require a lot of maintenance, and the work involved is often out of reach of most children, no matter how keen and dedicated. Some general rules of keeping fish are as follows:

- Choose your fish carefully. Don't choose on colour, but on how healthy they look. Select fish that are bright, alert and active. They should have a good appetite. Check for any signs of disease, such as spots, marks, or other injuries. Fins should be free of holes or wounds. The fish should be symmetrical — the left side should look the same as the right side. They should swim freely and not be hanging around the top or the bottom of the tank.
- Fresh water aquariums are easier to manage than salt water.
- Aquariums that require the water temperature to be higher or lower than the room temperature require a lot of effort. Tropical aquariums are an example and usually need water around 26–28°C (79–82°F).
- The larger the tank, the easier it is to keep under control. Smaller tanks obviously have less water which can quickly become polluted, undergo pH changes, or changes in temperature. So try to purchase the largest tank that suits you and that you can afford.
- The more species of fish, the greater the maintenance involved in keeping them all happy.
- The more fish in the tank, the harder it is to keep the tank clean.

The number one tip for fish is to look after the water. It's what keeping fish is all about. Filtration must be highly efficient at removing the waste from the tank water. Also, you should regularly check the pH and water temperature. In the case of saltwater (marine) aquariums, check the salt level by measuring the specific gravity. Any water changes must involve adding stabiliser to make the tap water liveable. Also, don't overfeed your fish. More fish die from eating too much than from eating too little.

Siamese Fighting Fish

The reputation of this fish precedes it; and probably a little undeservedly. They are originally from Southeast Asia, in particular Thailand (formerly known as Siam; hence the name). They gained their aggressive reputation from the fact that two male fighting fish in the one space will fight for dominance. It's an instinctive drive that comes from their origins, living in small bodies of water like small stagnant ponds and rice paddies, where they would have to fight for their territory and a mate. It makes sense then, that these fish are perfect for those people with little space. They require little ongoing maintenance and despite their name, are quite placid fish — provided they are left alone in their tank. The fighter is technically a tropical (warm, freshwater) fish, with 30°C (86°F) as their ideal temperature, but they will tolerate temperatures right down to 18°C (64°F). Anything lower than this and you will require a heater. While water quality isn't a big deal for these fish, regular water changes are still beneficial. The basic rule being the smaller the tank, the more frequent and drastic the water changes required. For a small bowl, try to change about a third of the water each week. In smaller containers, change the entire amount of water each week.

This fish will make a perfect first pet. The males are highly decorative and add life to any space around the house. And despite what you might think, you can add fighters to tanks containing other fish. Just avoid tanks with long-finned or red-coloured fish as these will be harassed. If solo, you can choose any sort of bowl to put them in, provided it's big enough for them to swim around in. But, as always with fish tanks, the bigger the better. Their adaptability comes from the fact they don't just rely on gills to breathe. They use an extra modification called a 'labyrinth' which sits in a chamber located above the gills. This enables them to absorb air gulped in through the mouth and survive in water that's stagnant and low in oxygen. Fighting fish are carnivorous, so they should be fed a commercial fish food or special pellets. Fresh bloodworms and mosquito larvae are a great extra treat. How much you feed is usually related to the water temperature. If it is warm, then feed a small amount each day. When it's cool you should feed less often.

CHEAT NOTES

- Don't put two male fighting fish together.
- This is a stunning fish that doesn't require stunning amounts of maintenance.
- The fish will be happiest in tropical conditions, but will cope with water at room temperature.
- Feed less in cooler conditions.

TIME: ★ SPACE: ★ COST: ★ EXERCISE: ☆ KIDS: ★★
NOISE: ☆ LIFESPAN: up to 2 years GROOMING: ☆ PERSONALITY: ★

Goldfish

The goldfish is probably the pet that takes the role of 'first pet' more than any other. And it's because people of all ages feel some degree of affection for them. Or is that sympathy? After all, the job description of a 'test-pilot pet' doesn't mention the danger, the risks and the long hours hoping that you haven't been forgotten. In reality, the popularity of the goldfish lies in their many attributes; of which one is certainly tolerance.

Although they originate from the common Asian carp, there are now more than 100 different types of goldfish. And you might be surprised just how far the goldfish has come. A huge variety of colours and styles are now available, making the humble goldfish not so humble after all. The new trend in goldfish has been towards the fancier varieties. These have features such as bulging or oddly-directed eyes, fluid-filled pockets around the eyes and mouth, lumps, bumps and crests which all add interest to their look.

Goldfish are hardy creatures, however, you can make it easier on them and yourself by setting up and maintaining their water-world the right way. For starters, try to get a large tank. Without an oxygenator, small bowls make it hard for a goldfish to get enough oxygen to survive. And in reality, larger bowls will save you time and money in the long-run, as filtration and ongoing maintenance is less draining. Once you've set up your tank or bowl, filled it with water, added the water stabiliser, and set up the filter, there's something left for you to do — nothing. Ideally, you should wait 2 weeks for the water to fully stabilise before you add your fish. In this time, concentrate on getting the water temperature right (ideally 21-24°C / 70-75°F, although they can tolerate 0-30°C / 32-86°F) and the pH correct (ideally 7.2, although they can tolerate between 6-8). Compared to other fish, the goldfish produces a lot of waste, so try to change around one third of the tank-water weekly, to stop the nitrogen levels building up.

The basic rule with goldfish is don't feed too much. Far more fish die from overfeeding than from underfeeding. Overfeeding is also a major contributor to poor water quality. To gauge whether you're feeding too much, check to see if any food remains after 5 minutes. If there is some food remaining, then drop off the amount.

CHEAT NOTES

- *Low maintenance compared to other fish, however, not as easy as their reputation suggests.*

- *They usually live up to 8 years, but up to 20 years is possible.*

- *Space the purchase of the tank and the purchase of the fish by up to 2 weeks. This allows the water to stabilise.*

TIME: ★★   SPACE: ★   COST: ★   EXERCISE: ☆   KIDS: ★★★
NOISE: ☆   LIFESPAN: up to 8 years   GROOMING: ☆   PERSONALITY: ★

Tropical Fish

How badly you want your own private reef under your roof will influence your choice of aquarium. The great thing about the tropical fish tank is that you still get colourful fish, but you may even get some time to enjoy them. The saltwater marine tanks are certainly spectacular, however, they can really stretch the meaning of the word 'hobby'.

The type and number of fish are obviously what is going to make the tank the feature it should be. But where do you start? There are hundreds of tropical fish species to choose from. At least to start with, why not make it easy for yourself. The best species are the tetras, angel fish, pencil fish, goramis, barbs, platies, hatchet fish, catfish and headstanders. These tend to be the most tolerant of changing water conditions. If you don't want to go 'troppo' like the fish, then avoid difficult species like discus fish, clown loach, elephant fish and anything that's going to be aggressive; and yes the piranha certainly fits into that category. Choose your fish carefully and (as mentioned earlier) go for the healthy, lively fish. Don't be blinded by beauty and introduce a sick, yet incredibly attractive fish. It won't be worth it in the long-run.

The key when choosing a home for your finned friends is to buy the largest tank that you can accommodate and afford. The smaller the tank, the quicker it pollutes and the more often you'll be changing the water and scrubbing it clean. Tap water is okay to use for fresh water tropicals provided it has been treated, de-chlorinated and the pH adjusted. The best temperature range for tropical fish is generally 28–30°C (82–86°F). You can find the right balance through using either a heater or a chiller, depending on the room temperature in your house, but always ensure the water never becomes too cold. In the same way as a cold shower is for us, low water temperatures in the tank are quite stressful to tropical fish. The other big factor is water pH. You'll need a pH test kit to keep a close eye on the acidity levels and while each fish has its own pH preference, a pH level of 5.0–6.0 is ideal. Getting the set-up and your water quality right is made even more crucial when you raise the temperature like is the case in a tropical world. Changes in the pH and water quality happen so much faster and problems can arise almost overnight.

CHEAT NOTES

- *Keeping tropical fish will take a lot of your time — a saltwater aquarium even more so.*

- *The bigger the tank, the easier it is to keep control of water quality, temperature and pH.*

- *Be smart with your choices of fish. Go with those that are easy as well as healthy.*

TIME: ★★★★ SPACE: ★ COST: ★★★ EXERCISE: ☆ KIDS: ★★
NOISE: ☆ LIFESPAN: 1–10 years GROOMING: ☆ PERSONALITY: varies, but ★

OTHER BEASTIES

Here's a group of creatures that don't seek out the spotlight — instead leaving it to their more flashy friends to hog the headlines. Yet they all make brilliant pets. It's certainly a mixed-up bunch — from the smallest of pets right through to one of the largest. As a posse, they've got every base covered. Each has its own special quality and its own unique attraction. They can live under the sea, beside the sea or far from the deep-blue, grazing a sea of green. And each is packed full of surprises. Which is part of the reason these pets are tailor made for kids — they seem to combine some freakiness with a major fascination factor. So many of these creatures would represent the perfect first step into the world of pets for those that are pint-sized and pet-obsessed. Kids can learn so much from these guys and then graduate onto something more complicated once they've earned their stripes in this section. Oh, and big kids might not complain about the fresh free-range eggs and homemade butter every morning too, if you decide to go a bit 'country'.

You don't have to be conventional when it comes to choosing a pet. You don't have to have a dog just because everyone in the street has one. Dare to be different. I've often found the best pets come from the most unexpected places and how you find them is all part of the fun. So throw away those inhibitions and take a wander through this unfamiliar farmyard — stopping to take in the scenery, the sights and the sounds. All you've got to do is give them a half a chance and they'll swim, scurry, hop and holler their way into your life — hopefully one at a time.

Hermit Crabs

Like Lego and lollies (candy), there is something about hermit crabs that fascinates kids. They are mysterious, shy little guys that seemingly everyone wants to know more about. But if you want to keep one, you have to make sure you choose and maintain their tank as well as they choose and maintain their own home — their shell. Unfortunately for the hermies sake, people often underestimate their needs. You pretty much have to condense a whole beach into their tank, so plan ahead. It doesn't have to be expensive but it does have to be well thought out. Start with a large rectangular fish tank and make a solid base of clean, dry (preferably beach) sand, about 5 cm (2 in) deep. Having a lid fitted to the top will aid in preventing any untimely escapes, but it will also keep the all-important humidity in. Next, it's time to set up the tank. You'll need two freshwater dishes (one for drinking and one for the crab to walk through and bathe in) that sit level with the sand. Clam shells give a natural look and store water well. The hermits love to scavenge for food, so leaving some small pieces of raw meat and vegetable around will satisfy any hunger pains.

Next, lets look at increasing the comfort levels for your little nipper. The temperature should be 24-27°C (75-81°F), so use an undertank heater if necessary. A high humidity level is needed to allow them to breathe properly, so use some damp, natural sponges around the tank, and a water mister spray to ramp up the tropical feel to their tank. Small pieces of driftwood, barnacles and shells also help to recreate that beachy feel. Finally, all hermits get itchy feet at some stage and want to upsize their little home. So provide a variety of real estate (new shells) around the tank whose openings are around 25 per cent larger than that of its current shell. After a moult, he will climb out of his old home and take up residence in the new abode.

If you are able to take care of each of these steps, you will be rewarded with a unique and interesting pet. But just as a reminder to the kids out there, this tropical Australian is pretty laid back, apart from one thing — whatever you do, just don't pull him out of his shell. Chances are he won't survive.

CHEAT NOTES

- *A fun pet for kids.*
- *Re-creating a suitable and natural environment is the most important thing. Make it a fun place for them to live. Warmth and humidity are all important.*
- *Supplementing the diet with calcium is a good idea. Use commercial supplements, sea shells and cuttle fish.*
- *Are more active at night.*

TIME: ★★ SPACE: ★ COST: ★★ EXERCISE: ☆ KIDS: ★★★★ NOISE: ★
LIFESPAN: up to 10 years GROOMING: ☆ PERSONALITY: ★ (hidden inside the shell!)

Sea Monkeys

For many of us, the first childhood encounter with the mysterious creature known as the Sea Monkey® remains clear. Clear like the water that was poured onto that magical powder to amazingly bring their aquatic paradise to life. In fact, in my neighbourhood, there were so many little underwater worlds of obedient 'monkeys' that my suburb was as close as you will ever get to a Sea Monkey solar system.

This is the magical instant pet. And to make it even more suited to the kids, this is pet ownership at its most simple. Just follow the instructions and add the magic powder (Sea Monkey eggs) to the purified water and out of your waterworld will slowly appear Sea Monkeys. Everything you need is contained in your Sea Monkey kit. The essential ingredients being the tank, water purifier and monkey food. What makes Sea Monkeys great though, is there is one essential ingredient missing from the kit. Imagination. And it's up to the kids to provide this by the spoonful. Who the tiny monkeys become and what their tank is transformed into is limited only by your kid's wildest dreams. Whether the monkeys' underwater world allows them to swim over the surface of the moon, among sunken pirate treasure or even on Mars is up to them.

There is one important rule that Sea Monkeys and their faithful trainers insist upon — never call them names. The most insulting is 'brine shrimp'. It's a word that would send shivers down their spine; if they had one. They know they're magical

and that's all that matters. You should always follow the instructions on your Sea Monkey kit exactly, but there are a couple of important points that will allow your Sea Monkeys to thrive.

Don't let the water get too cold or too hot. Water kept at room temperature is ideal. If they are too cold, then they become lazy, too hot and they become stressed and die. Give your Sea Monkeys some light, but not too much. Sunlight helps them to hatch and grow, but too much can be harmful. Indirect sunlight is safer than direct glaring sun.

Finally, if something does goes wrong and your Sea Monkeys die, there is a sneaky trick to bring them back to life. Simply let the water completely evaporate from the tank, then refill it with purified water. In a few days, a new batch of Sea Monkeys will start circling your tank once again.

CHEAT NOTES

- *The simplest pet on the planet.*
- *A great source of fun for big kids and little kids.*
- *Especially handy for teaching kids the basics of keeping a pet.*
- *Imagination is the most important ingredient.*

TIME: ★ SPACE: ★ COST: ★ EXERCISE: ☆ KIDS: ★★★★ NOISE: ☆
LIFESPAN: up to 2 years GROOMIING: ☆ PERSONALITY: depends on your imagination!

Mice

Despite what you might think, the tiny mouse is one powerful pet. After all, it has the power to make people love and look after it, but most commonly, it has the power to make people run, hide and shriek. But just pause for a while and take a moment to get to know this little character — he might just start to grow on you.

If those beady little eyes, snow-white whiskas, soft fur and pink tail don't do it for you, then how about I mention how easy it is to keep one as a pet? They make a perfect pet for kids who quickly grow to love them for their personality, as well as their unique ability to freak out their poor unsuspecting mothers. For around $2 you can buy a mouse, for $15 you can buy its house and for a few dollars a week you can keep it well-fed using mice cubes (a specially formulated mouse diet) and some occasional fruit and vegetables. Everything else they need for comfortable living can be found around the house —a small cardboard box for a bedroom, toilet roll for a toy, toilet paper for bedding — the only limit is your imagination and the size of their cage. Extra appliances for the mouse house, like an exercise wheel and ladders, are recommended to help keep your mouse active.

Mice make sociable and inquisitive little pets that enjoy human company and will (if you want them to) quite happily crawl from shoulder to shoulder and in and out of pockets. You are best to have two females together (two males can get smelly) in order to avoid your own mouse plague.

Mice unfortunately don't live long lives (up to 2-3 years), so love them while they are around. How clean and dry you keep their house plays a large part in keeping them healthy. A damp, dirty home is a breeding ground for nasty bacteria that can cause breathing problems as well as skin infections. You should always keep a lookout for lumps developing on your mice. Tumours are extremely common (especially on the belly), and can be fatal. The earlier they are detected the better, as some friendly vets may be able to remove the small ones and give your mouse a second chance.

CHEAT NOTES

- Not everyone's cup of tea, but give them a chance and you might find a mouse grouse.
- When picking up your mouse gently grasp it at the base of the tail and support it from underneath. Don't hold it too high when you're just getting used to each other.
- Choose a mouse that looks alert and active with bright beady eyes and a clean coat.
- Only buy mice from a breeder or a high-quality pet store that keeps its mice clean and healthy.

TIME: ★★ SPACE: ★ COST: ★ EXERCISE: ☆ KIDS: ★★★
NOISE: ★ LIFESPAN: 2-3 years GROOMING: ★ PERSONALITY: ★★★

Guinea Pig

Making a pig of yourself is something we all do at some stage. But what about having a full-time pig of your own. Their habits are cleaner and more decadent than your average sow, but you'll still get the odd squeal from time to time. I find the guinea pig an intriguing little fella — they'll eat and they'll squeak, all the while looking scarily like a living, breathing version of your uncle's toupee.

The guinea pig, which originally came from South America, can make a truly great first-time pet for kids. They have all the same requirements as a larger dog or cat, but on a much smaller scale. Like rabbits, housing and diet are the two essential elements in owning a 'pig'. Their little house should always be kept clean and dry, and out of direct sunlight, cold draughts, and in a place where you can regularly see them. Dining for a guinea pig must include large amounts of fibre. Fresh hay as well as guinea pig pellet mix will make up the bulk of the diet. Fresh vegetables (broccoli, spinach, cabbage, parsley) provide some nice variety. It's important to ensure there isn't too much fat in the feed (avoid sunflower seeds), as too much oil can cause skin and digestive problems. Having a large amount of fibre in the food stimulates them to chew, which is the important way they keep their teeth worn down, as their teeth grow continuously.

Most of the illnesses that the pig can come down with are due to either poor housing or diet — so that must be your first priority. Make sure you buy your little buddy from a high quality pet store or guinea pig breeder. If you start off on the right track, you have a great chance of keeping it that way. Diarrhoea (often due to a high fat diet and/or not enough fibre) and skin problems (fungal skin infections and mites) are the two most common issues.

CHEAT NOTES

- *The teeth grow continuously, so feed a high-fibre diet. An occasional teeth trim is often required.*

- *Keep the bedding dry and clean. Hay, straw or woodshavings make a good choice. Make sure the woodshavings are from untreated wood.*

- *Makes a great first pet and is handy to teach kids about pet care.*

TIME: ★★ SPACE: ★★ COST: ★★ EXERCISE: ★ KIDS: ★★★
NOISE: ★ LIFESPAN: 4–7 years GROOMING: ★ PERSONALITY: ★★

Dwarf Lop-Eared Rabbit

It's fair to say that not so long ago the rabbit suffered from a serious image problem. Those running free in the bush had been breeding like rabbits, and now had more offspring than they had burrows to keep them in. They were certainly under the spotlight, but a type of spotlight you didn't want trained upon you. But now, happily, with people being sensible about their rabbits, and measures in place to control the feral population, having a bunny can be a pleasurable experience.

The rabbit knows only two speeds: asleep while soaking up all the attention, or as fast as they can go. And you need to bear this in mind. Always act gently around them as sudden movements by you produce the same by them. When holding them, cushion them in your arms and hold them close to your body. This relaxes them, but also prevents any injury if they kick out from fear at any stage. When there is that element of trust there, they will be loving, attentive and relaxed pets. Although they will always be cautious around strangers. The dwarf lop is the pick of the domesticated species, as it combines a handy size with a settled temperament.

Having a rabbit isn't a huge drain on your time, provided you do the basics right. Have them desexed. This obviously prevents breeding but also makes them a more relaxed and friendly pet. In Australia, vaccinate against rabbit calicivirus. This is a virus that is used to control the feral population, and can infect your domestic rabbit just as easily. Ensure the housing is clean, dry and warm and regularly change the bedding. Hutches can vary in size, but a comfortable place to retire to is always nice. Watch for any signs of snuffles. This is a symptom of a disease that can kill rabbits if left unchecked. Look for runny or gunky eyes, sneezing, a runny nose and difficulty breathing. It's often a sign they are stressed due to the cold.

In the wild, rabbits are extremely active. However, city life is more about lazing around. So it's important you don't feed them too much, otherwise they will become fat. Fat rabbits can develop all sorts of skin problems, urinary and faecal-staining issues and infections. Feed rabbit food, not human food. Rabbits have a stomach that needs fibre, so make sure they get it by feeding a formulated rabbit pellet food and hay.

CHEAT NOTES

- *A daily brush is beneficial to remove dead hair.*

- *Treat them gently and do the basics right, and they can be a low-maintenance pet.*

- *They don't like open spaces (they tend to fret), so don't just leave them in the backyard.*

- *Avoid large breeds of rabbit. They tend to be higher maintenance and even aggressive.*

TIME: ★★ SPACE: ★★ COST: ★★★ EXERCISE: ★ KIDS: ★★★
NOISE: ★ LIFESPAN: 5–8 years GROOMING: ★★★ PERSONALITY: ★★

Okay, so it wasn't the first pet you had in mind. But show me another pet that can feed itself and then pays its own way with milk, butter, cream, cheese and ice cream. To me, our bovine buddies have always been the most fascinatingly brilliant animals I have ever laid my eyes upon. They are chilled out, chew cud, sleep standing up, and weigh 600 kg (1300 lb) and life couldn't be sweeter. If you're lucky enough to have the space for one, then I would go right ahead. You should look for a 'house' cow, which is a tame and friendly version of your standard cow. These have typically been hand-raised or brought up around people and have a definite social side. They will come when they are called and should enjoy a pat and a rub, especially behind their big paddle-like ears. You'll find them at either cattle sales (these are typically your more 'mature' cows), dairy farms, or sold from studs. When choosing a cow, the most important thing is to check the number of teeth. The less teeth she has, the less she can eat; which means her ability to produce milk and raise a calf is affected. Cows around 8-9 years have lost almost all their teeth; so aim for one younger than this (unless you like the idea of providing a nice retirement for an old girl).

The pick of the breeds is the Jersey, although Guernseys, Ayrshires, Brown Swiss and even the odd Friesian can fill the part. The best time to buy them is just after they have calved (given birth), so there will be a cheeky little moo-er running around as well as an abundance of milk. And it won't just be her calf that has a thick milk moustache.

Owning a cow means everything is on a large scale. Most notably the space you require and the food bills. Supplementary feeding with lucerne hay or dairy meal is often required, especially when she is producing large amounts of milk. However, make sure you don't feed her too many concentrates or lush clover as 'bloat' (where excess gas causes their stomach to swell) can be a serious problem. You'll also need to provide regular parasite protection and vaccinations. It's likely that one calf won't be able to drink all the milk on offer, so to stop her udder from becoming too full, it might help to milk her once or twice a day.

CHEAT NOTES

- Great to own but reserved for a lucky few that can.

- When choosing a cow, the most important thing is to check the teeth. Around 8-9 years, they have almost lost all their teeth, making it hard to feed themselves, as well as a calf. Older cows also need extra supplements.

- Ensure they don't just graze the one paddock. Rotate your cow between paddocks and drench often. This decreases the risk of worms.

TIME: ★★★   SPACE: ★★★★★   COST: ★★★★   EXERCISE: ☆ unless you like a rodeo
KIDS: ★★★   NOISE: ★★   LIFESPAN: 12–20 years   GROOMING: ★   PERSONALITY: ★★★★

Chickens

There's something romantic about the country. The relaxed way of life, its characters and, of course, its cruisy animals. Now, short of grazing a herd of herefords on your back lawn, a weekend away is usually the closest most people get to experiencing the country. That is until you invite a couple of hard working girls to stay that have but three interests in life — eating, drinking and laying. Bearing this in mind, I would be careful not to name your new chooks after your girlfriend, wife or mother.

This may be an appropriate time to introduce two special girls in my life. After all, who said three's a crowd? Juliet and Lucie strut around my back garden in the entirely non-rural setting of coastal Sydney. Sure, the neighbours are mystified by the gabble of a clucky hen as an egg is passed — but I reckon it just adds to the vibe of the area. A day in the life of the two girls isn't exactly gruelling, although I'd be reserving my energy too if I had to produce that oval-shaped object every morning. They are up with the sunrise but don't really get going until about 7 am, when the golden egg is laid. The rest of the day involves pecking around the garden, the odd roll in the dirt, an occasional squabble over a worm, an evening preen and feather manicure in front of their full length mirror before turning in at sunset.

People seem to think of chooks as being noisy, but nothing could be further from the truth. Remember that it's only the roosters that crow; so you won't be woken up at 4 am every morning. In reality, rarely has a pet given so much and asked for so little in return. For if you treat them nicely and shout them their dinner and a decent amount of space to peck and forage around in, you will be rewarded with a fresh, organic egg every day. The eggs taste great and will have rich, orange yolks if you supplement their normal diet with some left-over corn, lettuce and spinach.

You will need to make a pen that is fully enclosed to make it cat- and dog-proof. Chicken wire is called just that for a reason. Inside the chicken pen, you'll need at least one nesting box, with some straw or sawdust. Feed them laying pellets, which are available from your local pet supply store, as well as some fresh vegetables. Make sure there is always plenty of fresh, cool water to keep them hydrated as well as cool. They love to socialise, so let them out of the pen for at least a little while each day.

CHEAT NOTES

- Buy a 'laying' breed, not a 'broiler' or meat breed. There are some exotic species around now so look out for these.
- Worm them regularly.
- Learn how to hypnotise a chook — it's a great party trick.

TIME: ★★ SPACE: ★★★ COST: ★ EXERCISE: ☆ KIDS: ★★★★
NOISE: ★★ LIFESPAN: 5–6 years GROOMING: ☆ PERSONALITY: ★★

ANIMAL	time	space	cost	exercise
AUSTRALIAN MIST	★★	★★	★★	★
BICHON FRISE	★★★	★★	★★★★	★★
BIRMAN	★★★	★	★★★	★
BOXER	★★★★	★★★★	★★★★	★★★★
BRITISH SHORTHAIR	★★	★	★★	★
BURMESE	★★★	★★	★★★	★★
BURMILLA	★★	★★	★★	★
BUDGIE	★★	★	★	★
CANARY	★	★	★	☆
CAVALIER KING CHARLES SPANIEL	★★★	★★	★★★	★★
CHICKENS	★★	★★★	★	☆
DAIRY 'HOUSE' COW	★★★	★★★★★	★★★★	☆
DWARF LOP-EARED RABBIT	★★	★★	★★★	★
GOLDEN RETRIEVER	★★★★	★★★★	★★★★	★★★★
GOLDFISH	★★	★	★	☆
GREYHOUND	★★	★★★	★★★	★★
GUINEA PIG	★★	★★	★★	★
HERMIT CRABS	★★	★	★★	☆
LABRADOODLE	★★★★	★★★	★★★	★★★★
LABRADOR RETRIEVER	★★★★	★★★★	★★★★	★★★★
MALTESE X SHIH TZU	★★★★	★★	★★★	★★★
MICE	★★	★	★	☆
MINIATURE SCHNAUZER	★★★	★★★	★★★	★★★
MOGGIE	★★	★	★★	★
POODLE	★★★	★★–★★★★	★★★	★★–★★★
RAGDOLL	★★★	★	★★★	★
RHODESIAN RIDGEBACK	★★★★	★★★★	★★★★	★★★★
RUSSIAN BLUE	★★	★★	★★	★
SEA MONKEYS	★	★	★	☆
SIAMESE FIGHTING FISH	★	★	★	☆
SPOODLE	★★★★	★★★	★★★	★★★
STAFFORDSHIRE BULL TERRIER	★★★★	★★★	★★★	★★★
TROPICAL FISH	★★★★	★	★★★	☆
WHIPPET	★★★	★★	★★★	★★★

kids	noise	lifespan	grooming	personality	pages
★★★★★	★	★★★★★	★★	★★★★	186–187
★★★★	★★	★★★★	★★★★★	★★★	166–167
★★★	★★	★★★★	★★★★★	★★★	190–191
★★★★	★★	★★★★	★	★★★★★	170–171
★★★★★	★	★★★★	★★	★★★	188–189
★★★	★★★	★★★★	★	★★★★	184–185
★★★★	★	★★★★★	★★	★★★	182–183
★★★	★	★★★	☆	★★★	200–201
★★	★	★★	☆	★★	198–199
★★★★★	★★	★★★★	★★	★★★★	150–151
★★★★	★★	★★	☆	★★	224–225
★★★	★★	★★★★★	★	★★★★	222–223
★★★	★	★★★	★★★	★★	220–221
★★★★★	★★★	★★★★	★★★	★★★★	160–161
★★★	☆	★★★	☆	★	206–207
★★★	★★	★★★★	★	★★★	162–163
★★★	★	★★	★	★★	218–219
★★★★	★	★★★	☆	★	212–213
★★★★	★★	★★★★	★★★	★★★★★	168–169
★★★★★	★★★	★★★★	★★	★★★★	158–159
★★★	★★★	★★★★	★★★	★★★	154–155
★★★	★	★	★	★★★	216–217
★★★	★★★	★★★★	★★★	★★★	152–153
★★★	★	★★★★★	★★	★★–★★★	180–181
★★★	★★★	★★★★	★★★★	★★★–★★★★★	172–173
★★★★	★★	★★★★★	★★★★	★★★	194–195
★★★	★★★	★★★★	★	★★★	164–165
★★★	★	★★★★★	★	★★★	192–193
★★★★	☆	★	☆	☆–★★★★★	214–215
★★	☆	★	☆	★	204–205
★★★★	★★★	★★★★	★★★★	★★★★	176–177
★★★	★★★	★★★★	★	★★★★★	174–175
★★	☆	★★★	☆	★	208–209
★★★	★	★★★★	★	★★★	156–157

A

aggression, 87, 117, 126, 175
air sac mites, 199
allergies, 131, 186
antifreeze, 82
anus, redness, 124
anxiety, 83, 103, 117
aquariums, 202, 209
   water quality, 51
arthritis, 58, 64, 85
Australian mist (cat), 186-7

B

babies, and pets, 86, 103
Bambi, the black sheep, 20
barking, 52, 135, 139
bathing, 61-4
beds, 133, 135, 136
   cat, 138
   dog, 137
behaviour, rules, 45-7
belly, 123
'Beware of the Dog' sign, 52
bichon frise, 126, 166-7
birds, 55, 196
   holding, 134-5
   misting, 61
   preening, 61
   signs of illness, 50
birman (cat), 190-1
bite, 121
bloat, in large dogs, 60
boarding, 85, 128
bones, 74, 76, 139
boredom, 135, 139
boxers, 67, 170-1
Brad, friend of Chris, 28, 31
breathing, 123
breeders, 114-15, 118
Bridgette, the cow, 23, 29
British shorthair (cat), 188-9
Brown family, pets, 17-18
brushing, 65, 67
budgies, 196, 200-1

diet, 196
burmese (cat), 184-5
burmilla (cat), 182-3
burns, 80
Butch, the calf, 23, 29

C

calf, birth by caesarean, 20-2
calicivirus, 221
calving paralysis, 20
calving simulator, 29-30
camels, 67
canaries, 196, 198-9
   colours, 199
canine distemper, 56
cardiomyopathy, 25, 171
cars, 82
cat flu, 127-8, 131
cat training, 100
   digging, 103, 105
   no-go areas, 105
   scratching, 100
   territory disputes, 102-3
cats, 178
   anxiety, 55
   bathing, 61
   diet, 71
   fencing, 55
   getting along with dogs, 107-9
   grooming, 68-9
   hairless, 69
   scratching, 100, 140
   signs of illness, 50, 64
   strays, 181
   territory, 55, 102-3
   toilet use, 107
   travelling, 83
   vaccinations, 48
Cavalier King Charles spaniel, 126, 150-1
chemicals, 82
chest, 123
chewing, 138-9

chickens, 224-5
children, and pets, 86, 112, 133-4, 145, 146
chlamydia, 128, 131
chocolate, 74
choker chains, 59
choking, 80
circulation, 123
citronella oil, 139
Claude, the poodle, 19-20, 23, 24-6
coat, 123, 124
communication, 8-9
constipation, 190
coronavirus, 130
costs, 144-5
cows, 20, 222-3
crossbreeding, 147, 155, 168, 176
crying, at night, 139-40

D

dairy house cow, 222-3
dehydration, 50, 85
dependency, 136
desexing, 49
diarrhoea, 77, 124, 129-31
diet, 70-5
   change of, 131
   no-nos, 74
   picky eaters, 75
digging, 52, 103, 105, 117, 135
dog training, 88
   drop, 92
   high-5, 98
   okay, 96
   sit, 90
   stay, 94
dogs, 148
   bathing, 61-4
   diet, 70-1
   fencing, 52
   getting along with cats, 107-9

grooming, 67
heartworm, 48
shaking, 126
signs of illness, 50
throwing sticks, 58, 79
travelling, 83
vaccinations, 48
domestic shorthair cats, 180-1
dry food, 70
dwarf lop-eared rabbits,
    220-1

E

ears, 121-2
    ear hair, 65, 67, 172, 176
    ear mites, 48, 121
    infections, 63, 121-2, 151
    wax, 121
energy, 125
escaping, 139
exercise, 56, 58-60, 145
    and flat-nosed breeds, 59-60
    risk of disease, 56
eyes, 121, 122
    infections, 131
    sad eyes, 131

F

fairy penguin, rescue, 23-4
fans, cooling, 80
feather picking, 200
feeding *see* diet
feline infectious enteritis, 130
fencing, 52-5, 139
ferrets, 83
    vaccinations, 48
fireworks, 53, 139
fish, 145, 202
    signs of disease, 50
fish oils, 62
flat-nosed breeds, and exercise,
    59-60
fleas, 48, 49, 124
food wrappers, 76

G

games, 46-7
garbage eating, 76, 77, 130
gastroenteritis, 130
gender, 147
Glen and Jude, dairy farmers, 23
golden retriever, 122, 160-1
goldfish, 206-7
grass eating, 50
great dane, 144
greyhounds, 126, 144, 162-3
grooming, 64-9, 146
guinea pigs, 55, 218-19
    bathing, 61
    bite, 121

H

hair, singeing, 80
hair loss, 64, 124, 160
hairless cats, 69
health checks, 119
heartworm, 48
heat stroke, 59
hermit crabs, 212-13
hernias, 123
hip dysplasia, 159, 160
holding a pet, 134-5
holidays, 83-5
home-coming, 133-41
house cow, 222-3
Hunter Valley farm, 20
hybrid vigour, 155, 168

I

illness, 50-1, 118
introduction, to a dog, 87

J

Jersey Cow Conference, 22
Jersey cows, 22

K

kennel cough, 56
kneecaps, slipping, 122

L

labradoodles, 168-9
labrador retriever, 122, 145,
    158-9
large dogs
    bloat, 60
    growth diet, 73
lead paint, 82
leash, 58
    pulling on, 59
legs, 122, 123
lifespan, 146
lilies, 79
limping, 58
litter trays, 100, 103, 106, 133
long-coated dogs, 67

M

maltese x shih tzu, 154-5
mature animals, 147
medications, 81
Merewether Heights, 17
Merv, the calf, 21-2, 29
mice, 216-17
Mick, farm manager, 39-40
microchips, 52, 139
miniature schnauzer, 152-3
misbehaviour, 47
mites, 48
Mittens, the moggie, 18-19
Mittens Circus, 18-19
moggies, 180-1
mouth, 120
mouthing, 126
muzzles, 163

N

nail trimming, 69, 100, 140
name tags, 139
Narellan Poultry Auctions,
    31-2, 33
neutering, 49
Neutral Bay Vet Clinic, 31
Nip, the kelpie, 34

noise, 145-6
nose, 120
nuts, 74

O

oils, skin, 62
omega-3, 62
onions, 74
overeating, 130

P

panting, 59, 123
paralysis ticks, 48, 85
parvovirus, 56, 129
pecking order, 145
pedigrees, 114-15, 147
Penny, the boxer, 15-17, 19
Percy, the pelican, 17-18
personality, 146
pet inspection, on-site, 120-4
pet ownership, benefits, 7-9
pet profiling, 125-7
pet selection, 112-19
   criteria, 144-7
pet stores, 116, 118
pets, holding, 134-5
Phantom, 27, 28-9
Phantom Carers' Society, 29
picky eaters, 75
plants, poisonous, 78-9
play, 46-7
play-biting, 126
poisons, 82
Poo-Cat, 106, 138
poodles, 67, 126, 172-3
pounds, 117, 126-7
power cords, 81
purebreds, 114-15, 147

R

rabbits, 83
   bathing, 61
   bite, 121
   digging, 55

dwarf lop-eared, 220-1
   vaccinations, 48
ragdoll (cat), 69, 194-5
responsibility, 7-8, 135
rhodesian ridgeback, 60, 164-5
ringworm, 124
Romper Room, 15-16
Rosie Brown, the dog, 34-7,
39, 40, 61, 68, 77, 84, 136-7
rough-coated dogs, 67
Russian blue (cat), 69, 192-3
Rusty, the dog, 38-41, 77

S

safety, 76, 78-82, 86
scaly face mite, 200
scratching, 100, 140
scratching post, 140
Sea Monkeys, 214-15
selection criteria, 144-7
separation anxiety, 126, 175
shampoo, for dogs, 64
short-coated dogs, 67
siamese fighting fish, 204-5
sickness, 50-1, 118
silky-coated dogs, 67
skin, 124
   allergies, 186
   mites, 48
   oils, 62
sleeping quarters, 135-7, 138
Slobber Chops, 15-17, 19
small dogs, knees, 122
Snoopy, the cat, 24
socialisation, 56, 86, 94, 109,
   116
   risk of disease, 56
socks/underwear, 76
spicy foods, 74
spoodles, 176-7
spotted mist (cat), 186-7
Staffordshire bull terrier, 60,
   67, 174-5
stove tops, 81, 105

stray cats, 181
string, 76
sunburn, 85, 156

T

tapeworms, 130
tear ducts, blocked, 131, 167
tear staining, 65
teeth, 120-1, 122
teething, 79, 80, 138-9, 147
terriers, 144
territory disputes, 55, 102-3
thunderstorms, 53, 139
ticks, 48, 85
toilet training, 105-7, 133,
   140-1
toys, 76, 80, 135, 139
training, 88-107
travelling, 83-5
treats, 74
tropical fish, 208-9
tumours, mice, 217

U-Z

under-bite, 155
urine spraying, 103, 145
vaccinations, 48, 56, 118, 128
Veterinary Science course, 26,
   29-30
vomiting, 77
walks, 56, 58
Wandering Jew, 79
weight gain, 73, 76
weight loss, 76
whimpering, 136, 137, 139-40
whippets, 126, 156-7
Winnie, the cow, 22, 23, 29
wire-coated dogs, 67
worming, 48, 118
worms, 123, 130
Zac, the labrador, 33

THANK YOU

A much deserved (and probably overdue) thank you must go to Mum for letting me get these stories out before she ever did and cheers to Dad for exposing me to the world of animals from such a young age — I think it was a good thing. Thanks also to Jet for her support, to Sean for his belief in the concept and to the whole Murdoch Books team for their energy and encouragement. A big 'respect' must go to the Goonies — for keeping it real, of course. I would also like to apologise to any pet mentioned in this book, whose reputation may never be the same again.

Murdoch Books would like to thank the following people for their assistance in the photography of this book:
Monique and Ross Baxter, Tracey Bradbury, Natasha Castro, Davide and Sophia Cece, Maggie and John Chambers, Petrina Convey, Cristina Custodio, Lindsey Forrest, David and Kylie Haas, Jenny Hansen, Emma Hutchinson, Daniel Joyce, Brielle Koolen, Denise Mackenzie, Georgia and Kate Macquire, Amanda McKittrick and Daniel Bogan, Kylie Mulquin, Marion Neal, Darrell O'Loughlin, David Ritzau and Rodney Hodder, Stephen Ryan, Kay Scarlett, Gayle Smyth, Tiani Vanderberg, Jaki Wallbank, John and Natalie Watson, Rhiain Hull and Mark Watson, and Ed Westhead and Don Stewart.

Also, thank you to: Aquapets Aquariums, Pets Paradise, Pet Addiction, Raw Hair Sydney and Strictly Pets.

Published by Murdoch Books Pty Limited

Murdoch Books Pty Limited Australia
Pier 8/9, 23 Hickson Road, Millers Point NSW 2000
Phone + 61 (0) 2 8220 2000 Fax + 61 (0) 2 8220 2558

Murdoch Books UK Limited
Erico House, 6th Floor North, 93–99 Upper Richmond Road, Putney, London SW15 2TG
Phone: + 44 (0) 20 8785 5995   Fax: + 44 (0) 20 8785 5985

Chief Executive: Juliet Rogers
Publisher: Kay Scarlett

Design Manager: Vivien Valk
Project Manager and Editor: Paul McNally
Design concept: Jacqueline Duncan
Designers: Michelle Cutler and Sarah Odgers
Photographer: Suzie Mitchell
Photographer's Assistant: Nigel Lough
Production: Megan Alsop

National Library of Australia Cataloguing-in-Publication Data:
Brown, Chris, Dr. The family guide to pets. Includes index. ISBN 1 74045 593 2.
1. Pets — Handbooks, manuals, etc. I. Title. 636.0887

Printed in China by SNP Leefung Printers Limited